The Alphabetized Job Search

By
Joan Addison
and
Dale S. Liebman

ISBN-10: 1456439944
ISBN-13: 978-1456439941

The Alphabetized Job Search

TABLE OF CONTENTS

INTRODUCTION	1
A (Activity - Attitude)	3
B (Baggage - Busy)	13
C (Calendar - Credit Checks)	20
D (Dates - Dueling for Jobs)	29
E (Easy - Extra)	36
F (Failure - Funny Names)	40
G (Ganging Up - Gut)	46
H (Hand Shake - HR)	51
I (Identity Theft - Inventions)	55
J (Jerks - Justify)	58
K (Kindness - Know Thy Self)	63
L (Landing - Luck)	65
M (Magic - Murphy's Law)	68
N (Name - Notice)	74
O (Offer - Oxymoron)	77
P (Paper - Professionalism)	80
Q (Qualifications - Quickly)	86
R (Rambling - Rules)	88
S (Search Engines - Surprises)	97
T (Telecommuting - Tweet)	108
U (Urban - Under-qualified)	116
V (VC's - Volunteer)	118
W (Wages - Wreckage)	121
X (Xerox Copies - X-Ray)	127
Y (Yacht Interviews - Young)	128
Z (Zebra - Zoo)	130
INDEX	I

INTRODUCTION

Welcome to this unique and hilarious book, "The Alphabetized Job Search", which will add insight, coupled with levity, to your job search quest. "The Alphabetized Job Search" is a one-of-a kind book that will help you be better prepared on your mission to find another job. Career books, along with resume writings and all the how-to-books, definitely add knowledge to your repertoire. However, "The Alphabetized Job Search" book is unique, and sets itself above the rest, because of the real life experiences that have happened to actual job seekers, much like you, looking for their next job. Finding another job becomes just that, a job in finding a job! You will find yourself immersed in real life situations and experiences as you scan each page. This book introduces you to the eye-opening world of job search.

The realism is expounded throughout the alphabetized vignettes. You will read, perhaps be a little surprised, of what may happen in various situations, and laugh because some of the stories are just plain funny!

Remember when life was simple? When having a chocolate mocha made everything okay? Remember when worries were not part of your life? This book will help you bring your worries to an acceptable level. This book will bring you the ways and means of finding your next job. Can you remember the very first time you had to learn something, let's say, swimming? With your first attempt you thought you were going to drown. However, after learning how to keep afloat, you realized that with each stroke you became more adaptable to the water. That is what "The Alphabetized Job Search" brings to you.

The Alphabetized Job Search

With your first Alphabetized Job Search stroke, you will gain more and more insight. Sit back, take the plunge, and be ready to learn the art of the Job Search!

To quote a very old and wise Chinese Proverb, "The hardest part of the journey is the first step". Your first step has begun because YOU are reading "The Alphabetized Job Search". Your end goal, finding a job, is getting the job you want. Mind you, not just any job, but THE job that would energize you. One that stimulates your thoughts puts a smile in your heart as well as on your face. You will realize that it is possible to find your dream job by understanding the game you are now playing using logic and clear direction.

How many times have you heard people say, "He/She was lucky"? Luck has nothing to do with Job Search.

The format of "The Alphabetized Job Search" is as simple as the English alphabet. We designed this for you to have fun and laugh as you take on your wonderful adventure. As you read through our Alphabet, you will be able to connect with the various activities in your Job Search venture. Remember when you began a new job and the Trainer told you to ask any question that you might have? If you knew the right question to ask, you would not have needed the Trainer! Using this A through Z digest, you will be prepared for the usual and unusual job search situations. This Digest will help you answer the unanswerable questions and provide the answers with a very easy format. We designed this to lead you through each nuance of your Job Search. Under each letter of the alphabet, you will understand, and become knowledgeable, about your Job Search adventure. You will become savvy about the various strategies.
Good Luck on your Job Search! We sure hope that you will find your next dream come true job!

A

Activity

So what? I sent one thousand resumes, went on hundreds of interviews, took many profile tests, and still nothing. Think of this as a slot machine in Las Vegas. How many people put in thousands of coins in a slot machine to see absolutely nothing, nadda, in return? Why? How can I change this? Can I change this? Of course you can change this! You are the master of your ship! You have heard the expression, "Work Smarter, Not Harder"? It is the beginning of your job search. You will be smarter because you will adapt to the new world of Job Search. If you have never enjoyed metrics, do not apply for jobs that require reports that will take up 90% of your workday. By understanding what functions energize you, you can have a great beginning for your job search. Instead of sending thousands of resumes out to Industries, and/or organizations not of your desired work, focus on your activities and interests. Any activity that takes up your job search time should be focused with "you" in mind. Use your job search wisely. Stay energized and please do not lose your humor.

Ads

Help needed, help wanted – Help-----!!! ☺☺☺
Did you ever think about Advertising Ads? On second thought have you ever seen Advertising Ads? Do you really believe in what you are being sold? Of course you do, that's why you buy products. Advertising is a wonderful thing especially if you are the advertiser! You are the buyer and that puts you in another category. You have heard many times, "Let the buyer beware!" This is not a trite

statement. Should you answer a job ad that appears to be 'too good to be true', then the ad is too good to be true! Before signing up for anything, please read all the fine print. Or if the fine print is too very small – don't bother with it unless you are willing to sell your next born. Should an Ad request your credit card number that should immediately send you a red flag. Not every ad has evil behind it, just be cognizant of what you are agreeing to after signing your name on the dotted line, assuming you can read that fine, not so fine, print.

Age

Hide it. Leave it in your car. Chronological Age, whether you are younger or older, can be either positive or negative. The age of the organization you are interviewing with can have a lot to do with how well you will fit. Let's face it; we live in a visual society. Just remember that no matter whatever your age, if what you bring to their table is much desired, your age should not be an issue. This must be your plan. It is so easy for those who are young to feel that they didn't get their job because they were not experienced enough and therefore were under qualified. It is also very easy for those who are older to feel that they are "over qualified" because their pay history was too high, etc. It's very easy to blame not getting the position to age, too young or too old. Do you really think that was the reason? If you were to take your age out of the equation, was that really the reason you did not receive a job offer? Be honest and turn that 'young old' scenario around. Be energized and maximize your strengths on showing the Hiring Manager why YOU are truly the best candidate. You have heard, "When life throws you lemons, make it into lemonade". It's your turn to make some great lemonade. Super person is here to save the day! Age is real, you have it and it is here to stay, but you can turn that around and prove to the Hiring Manager that you, indeed, are the best candidate.

Agenda

Yours, or theirs?

Your agenda is most important to you. However, those empowered folks who have the authority to hire and fire, their agenda is most important to them! Therefore, their Agenda should become your Agenda! Your handling them must be dealt with a win-win attitude on your behalf. OUCH! They need to fill a position and the hiring process is very painful to them. They know that they have to put the right person at that desk. If you address their pain by stating how you can fix their pain, well, there you go…win-win! Having the criteria needed for the job function isn't the only thing that Hiring Managers are stressing. It is also very important for you to fit in with their team. By doing your homework and learning as much as you can about the Company, you will have a wonderful idea as to what their environment is. Remember, their Agenda is paramount. Your Agenda must be presented in such a way that your Agenda is their Agenda.

Agreeable

Better to help your personality somewhat by being positive, rather than negative. Think about your discussions with folks when they are negative. If they become somewhat agreeable, your face puts on a smile. Remember this thought especially when you are interviewing for a position. An agreeable reply is more tasteful that being argumentative. This is a job interview and not a debate.

Allergies

"Gezundheit" may prove to be the first word that is said in your interview! Wouldn't it be awful if your interviewer had a sneezing attack during your interview? This can really happen if you are wearing perfume, after-shave, colognes, etc., that they are allergic to. When in doubt – leave it out. Bring tissues just in case.

Analyze

No, you're not visiting a Therapist! However, you will do this a lot in your Job Search as you compare your today with your imagined tomorrow. You have a job and are lucky that your employer has promoted you and treated you like family. Then your friend tempts you with thoughts of opportunities to make money. What do you do? As you go on these interviews what do you ask? What do you look for? The best analysis tool you can use is one piece of paper, having two columns. The first column would be, "YES", and the other column would be, "NO". Write down every possible yes or no and then take a step backwards and see which column has more written under it. Analysis can often prove to be very subjective. If your heart is leading you towards a specific decision that may well be your right decision! Have faith in your feelings! We are so much smarter after we know all the facts! How many times have you played, "Monday morning quarterback"? We always know the answers after the game was played. Let's take Jeff, for example. He had a very secure position, working in his field. He had been promoted several times over a short period of time, and his earnings were continually increased. He was not at all being considered to be one of those employees to be downsized. However, Jeff just was not fulfilled in his job and therefore sought for greener pastures. Unfortunately, his focus began with green as in money greener pastures. After, a few short weeks at his new job he realized that was not everything.

Anger

These feelings may be there for you. It could be that you are still angry with a previous boss, angry that you were laid off or just angry that your interviewer made you wait. Hide these feelings! Most of all don't let your interviewer find them. You will be tested big time! Your interviewer will be testing your stamina when they make you sit in the lobby all by yourself for 45 minutes after flying in for the interview. Nowhere to go and the next and last flight out is in 2 hours.

Animals

Not the human kind, but our furry friends! We love our furry creatures. Now, with that being said, what do we do when we are on a telephone interview and our little precious is barking so loud that it sounds as though you were beating this poor thing? You should put little precious in a comfortable environment, with food and water and not so close that the interviewer thinks you are an axe murderer! Don't be surprised if your furry kids decide to sit on the papers on your desk during your phone interview if you let them be in the same room. Other experiences that can happen during your phone interviews can be when your cat slips and falls off a railing down 20 feet. Just scream and see what happens to your interviewer on the phone. This will take a new direction for you and you will gain control over the interview. It's amazing what embarrassment your mute button can save you! "Be prepared" for any circumstance when you have pets! Whether your dog decides to bark, your cat decides to demand attention, perhaps your doorbell is ringing, remember; just be prepared for the unexpected.

Applications

Beware as to how much of your privacy you are willing to give away! You will be amazed at what employment applications ask for. Government applications ask for the world. They will ask you to put down every job you ever had in your life, dates, salaries, addresses, etc. If you aren't able to provide all of this information dating back to

1901, then don't be afraid to ask them what they suggest you do. They will ask for dates for almost everything. Legally they can't ask for the dates you attended High School. So what! They can ask you to put how many total years of work experience you have and the dates you attended college. DAH! They will also ask you to sign your life away for them to research your background. Never give your date of birth to an employer until after you start your job. Just remember when filling out an application, "Tell the Truth"! In our electronic age, a prospective employer can find out just about anything there is to find out! If you stick to the truth you won't have to be worried about being found out if you stated something incorrectly. Would you want to hire someone if you found out they were not being honest on their Application? Of course not!

Apple

An apple a day keeps the Doctor away! The very first thing one needs to do is stay healthy. By staying healthy this doesn't just mean physically, it also means emotionally, spiritually and mentally. To begin your Job Search all these things must be lined up and ready for your big serge of finding a new job. Having your apple is the beginning of your new search.

Applying

For jobs via electronic, e-mail, snail mail, in person and/or fax. Applying for a job opportunity can be very exciting and invigorating. A new hope, a new possibility, a new day, hopefully, a new job! Whoa…pull those reins tighter. You are applying for a new job and you feel as if you are on the biggest roller coaster ride of your life. No matter what venue you are utilizing, you must focus on what is being requested, presuming you have the credentials – say what?? If you have the criteria in meeting the position's needs, address those needs.

It's not important to the Hiring Manager if the job meets your needs. What is important is that you meet what they need. Forget about your basic needs, which are food. If you are able to keep this in mind, your application will be read. A generic resume, not addressing you, your ability and capability, will not help you with your application. If you remain focused on your direction, in conjunction with your experience, your application will fit the opportunities you seek. Okay, so maybe you want to plant flowers instead of selling flowers. Your resume needs to reflect that you can reap what you sow. When all else fails just go smell the roses. Address the needs in your cover letter regarding what the open position is requesting and your resume and application will have a good chance of actually being read.

Are

This little 3-letter word can be a big one in a job interview. Are you still working? When are you available? Are you able to travel? Are you willing to sell your soul for your next job? Are you in need of tranquilizers to help you get through the day? Are you ready for a possible change that will alter your life for the better? Are you thinking that change might be just what 'the Doctor ordered'? Perhaps this might be as good a time as any to take stock in where you are, physically, emotionally, and spiritually. Ever hear the adage, "Can't see the Forest from the trees"? Maybe now would be a great time for you to regroup internally and in a quiet corner answer all the, "Are you", questions. You might surprise yourself, in a very positive way, by taking the time to reflect where you have been and where you want to be. Perhaps this might be the best time for you to make a change for the better. You can then wonder why it took you so long to get to the emotional place you are at. You might just prove to yourself that change isn't so bad after all and your tomorrows will prove to be better then you ever anticipated. Are you ready to alter your life for the better? Perhaps now is the best time for you to do that!

Art

Ever thought you had creative talents? Not feeling like a Rembrandt, Van Gogh, or Picasso? You will be shocked after you realize that you are in the "The "ART" of Job Search"! For centuries, the artisans provided pictures in their various venues, oil, pastel, etc. Comparing art in the visual sense can be combined with the art of acquiring a job. The "ART" of Job Search is learning the "how" for you to go about preparing the proper canvass and fine-tuning the canvass into the final picture that would prove to be your finest production. Picasso wore many faces and so can you, as you endeavor down this road. As the Artisans used many different styles, you, too, will see that tuning your personality to your Job Search will be as individual as each Artist uses their individual talents to present their finest works.

Assess

Working on a puzzle, with too many parts, sometimes isn't fun! For those who have started anything, whether it is a jigsaw puzzle or building a home, what's the most important part of these accomplishments? If you are saying, "PLANNING", you win! Planning is the most important part of beginning anything. In order to facilitate your end-result, you must assess what it is you want, and then plan how you will arrive at your desired end-result. Assessing can be as easy or as hard as you make it. If you want to be a Rocket Scientist, you must assess the planning stage to the Moon or Mars. If you haven't lived there before, realize that higher learning will be in your future. Assessing what your end result is, you can take a blue-line, also known as a legal pad, and write down all the things that you will need to focus on to achieve your end result. You may conclude that your desired end result will be too arduous a journey. It is up to you to determine how grandiose your dream is and how you can implement it within realistic expectations. What do you want to be when you grow up? Nothing? Now what? Are the areas under the road over pass bridges congested with no place to set up your camp? If so, not to worry! Believe it or not, this is the best time for you. You are now saying, "You've got to be kidding"! The best time is now to finally give yourself an introspective as to who you are as a person, where you have been, and where you truly want to be. You might not know all the answers, but you know what you like. You like vanilla, not chocolate. What, not chocolate? Sorry, we're getting away from the point here. Can you picture a perfect day at work or are you saying that's an oxymoron? You know where you want to be…let's say, going to a job everyday with your workday ahead of you, doing work you actually enjoy. After doing your assessment of what floats your boat, creatively think of what you really can do. What environment you can live with that will not only allow yourself to pay your bills but would also give you the quality of life you long for and never were able to attain.

Attitude

Don't assume that all might be just crap because a couple of your interviews were just not what you expected. You have to kiss a lot of frogs before you find your prince or princess! Remember, it only takes ONE position to answer your dreams. Your attitude needs to be positive and upbeat. Picture yourself as the interviewer. How would you react to interviewees who are emotionally down, depressed, and not energized? Would you choose them as your perfect candidate for your open position? Probably NOT! You can control your attitude! Picture your paradise, sunny blue skies, with birds chirping and Mother Nature in full bloom, whatever. While thinking all those beautiful thoughts, your attitude has to be positive and that's exactly how you want to portray yourself to any Hiring Manager! Should you find your attitude not where you want it to be, change the channel! When you are watching a television program and don't like what you're watching, you change the channel don't you? You have the power of the remote control right in your mind and you have the power to change bad thoughts to good thoughts, all within your scope of having a positive mental attitude - PMA!

B

Baggage

Leave your baggage at home! You are beginning new challenges. If you choose to hold on to the negatives, all you will be left with are more negatives. Think about the positives, the good stuff in your life, the people you enjoy being around. That is what your prospective Hiring Manager wants to see. Why would the Hiring Manager want you if all you brought were negatives to his/her table? The answer is, "They wouldn't". Leave your baggage behind and brace yourself for positive results. On the other hand, if your baggage can fit under the seat on an airplane you may be okay.

Begging

"Buddy, can you spare a dime?"

People tend to cheer for the underdog, but somehow they don't when the situation arises when you are seeking your next position and begging for that job. Begging brings out the feelings of desperation. Put this into focus. When your cat or dog begs - they get a wonderful treat. They make you feel guilty and sorry. Hiring Managers don't want to feel sorry for you so avoid getting them into that mode in your job search. Their mission is to hire someone who is right for the job. Leave your begging, your dog, and cat at the door, and walk in with a positive demeanor. Sure and steady will win that bone!

Beginning

In the?? ☺☺ Adam and who? Are they a public company? What is their product? A "what" leaf? How many times have you heard, "the hardest part of the journey is the first step"? Sometimes beginning is difficult due to many reasons. It's possible to begin your journey and then have fear of the unknown that then makes you immobile. The more knowledge you have in Job Search, the more confident you will become. Pretend you were talking to someone and you were giving them a positive feeling about their new endeavors. Can you pretend that the person you are giving the positive feed back is yourself? Yes you can be successful if you just begin the process. "YES" should be your mantra. You're good!

Behavioral Questions

Oh, oh, here comes the human dynamics with, "what's your birth sign"! You will have behavioral questions in interviews and be quite amazed at what they ask. Your clue might be if they say we believe past behaviors are indicative of future behaviors. Don't run under the conference table. You can handle these questions. What would your answer be if you were asked, "What is your philosophy on life"? Or if you are a sales person looking for a job and were asked, "What is your philosophy on sales"? Or you are older than dirt and they say, "Tell me about High School", "Tell me about your first job", "Give me an example about a problem you once solved", "Tell me about a time you were criticized", "Give me examples of how you handled working on a project with a customer that never seemed to be satisfied. What did you do and what would you do differently now"? Don't start sweating – it will show. Ask for further clarification if you need it. These are very broad open-ended questions. That is your interviewer's plan. You can mention that you realize that there is limited time and you want to utilize it to everyone's best advantage.

Believe

In yourself and your dream and keep on keep on trucking. It will come true. There is much to be said on the power of belief. "Wishing" will make it so! This philosophy has won over many folks who question the power of thought. If you choose not to believe in yourself, then who will? It's now time for you to become your own best friend. Your beliefs, of what and who you are as a person, are critical for your quest with finding a great job. If you can't sell yourself on who you are, how would you possibly sell a Hiring Manager on how great you are? Your beliefs, of what you bring to the table, are paramount in your achieving your successes. Believe in yourself, front and foremost, and you will have set up a scenario of "win-win" for not only you but for your future employer. Believing in yourself will go a long way in achieving your goals.

Be Prepared

All you have learned from Boy Scouts, Girl Scouts, sometimes known as People Scouts or whatever, is now going to play a major role in your life today. Think back to when you first went to school and you forgot your lunch money, or your pencil, or your homework. Not being prepared left you with more embarrassing moments than you care to remember. Be Prepared! Have your i's dotted and your t's crossed while on your Job Search. Your preparation, with all your endeavors, will lead you to your course of action, which will be your next job. Think through all those what if's prior to the interview.

BIAS

Prejudice happens. If your Hiring Manager is thin, and you are not, it's not their fault that they can wear a belt and you can't! People are biased for various reasons. Ensure that you don't talk about your children, your Religious beliefs, and your political affiliation or anything that could be misconstrued by the Interviewer. Stick to the discussions regarding the job function. Don't throw yourself out of the ball game because of your personal beliefs or lifestyle. Be cognizant that there probably will be differences between your beliefs and the beliefs of the Hiring Manager. Think of this as dating and this is your first date.

Bizarre

Some of your interviews and questions can only be described this way. They will be just plain strange and unusual. Companies take pride in creating such an interview environment. They will ask off the wall questions to test your creative and analytical skills.
For example:
Why is a manhole cover round? If you are going to receive an award in 5 years, what is it for and who is the audience?
What color is the moon and why?
The purpose of these questions is to bring, to the front, your creative and quick thoughts that will be needed on the job.

Blitz

What in the world is a Blitz interview? How do I prepare? Is this helping me? If so, how? Is this another gimmick scam? How can I differentiate what is a scam in my Job Search World? Often Blitz interviews are done at events such as Job Fairs or College Recruitment. This can give you that one precious moment to shine. Sometimes companies who have high turnover jobs conduct Blitz Interviews because it is just a turnstile numbers game for them. The dictionary definition for Blitz is: "Informal, a sudden, energetic, and concerted effort, typically on a specific task". Be positive and keep your eyes wide open.

BLOGS

Are everywhere. They are your story and can be used as your marketing tool. They can also be utilized against you. Look at your Blog from a prospective employer's view. Anything published on the Internet about you is available for all to see. Do a search on yourself and see what you find. Guess what? If you can find it anyone else can.

Boring

You or your Interviewer? What do you say when the interviewer can't stop yawning while you are speaking? You could ask, "Would you like to continue this meeting after your nap?" "Should we continue our interview at Starbucks?" The one thing that you can control is your sense of humor! When all else fails, laugh! Believe it or not, sometimes the interviewer is not focusing on you at all! It could have been a very long night for him/her, "Sleepless in Seattle", or where ever, is not unusual for an interviewer. It could be that it's not you who is boring, but rather, your interviewer is bored! Maybe they just plain hate their job. Can you turn this situation around? You bet! Here's where your creativity and outgoing personality can shine! If you give this your best shot and your interviewer is still yawning, the embarrassment on your interviewers face speaks volumes. You might say, "Interviewing for this position has probably been quite tedious for you. Perhaps you have found your perfect candidate, "ME", and you won't have to continue your interviewing monotony."

Breathe

I breathe therefore I am hired. Watch out for these opportunities. Often they will be commission only, no benefits types of sales jobs. Their products will be the best thing since "Sliced Bread". When in doubt, leave it out.

Breathing

Please don't stop! Just be careful not to breathe directly into your phone during a phone interview. The hiring manager may think that you have become an obscene caller. Hyperventilating is a possibility when anxiety prevails. Running late to your interview can bring on some heavy chest action as well. Here's where your knowledge of deep breathing exercising will come in handy. Take a deep cleansing breath, then another, and then another still. Slow down! Get back to that old self! There is nothing wrong by you saying something short and sweet to set the tone of your interview. You can break the tension by offering something clever so you and your interviewer can laugh, or even smile! This isn't the Olympic tryouts? Dang! Once the tone is changed, your breathing will become more normalized and you can then focus on addressing your interviewer's questions.

Bullet Points

A bullet, not to your head or heart! Done wrong they can be like bullets in your side. Be brief, concise and put them in the order according to that which you want the prospective employer to focus. On your resume, where you have aligned your documented experience, use these bullets to your advantage. You have captured the attention of the reader. The beginning bullet points will be what your reader peruses and those bullet points should capture what the specific job entails. You will have just a few seconds for the reader to read your Resume and if you utilize this methodology, by putting your bullet points strategically placed on your Resume, you will prove to the reader that you are a good candidate for their open position. As you prove your position of experience, with each bullet comes more proof for the Reader that you are a viable candidate. The lesson learned here is that your bullets need to prove a strong case for you being their perfect candidate!

Business Plan

An interview requirement – for you to use or for them? Business 101…have a plan! What better test for you than to ask for a Business Plan from your Interviewer? Or you may be asked to present a business plan to them as part of your interview process. The Business Plan helps separate the novices from the highly skilled. Remember, you are seeking a position to take the pain away from your perspective employer. You walk in with a Business Plan that will 'knock 'em dead' and you've already passed the hurdle of, "Can you perform the tasks?" This could also be a great way for your perspective employer to achieve more Business Plan ideas! Don't forget to put your name, and reach information, on each page. You don't want them to accidentally give another candidate credit for your ideas. After all, they are probably receiving plans from at least five or more candidates.

Busy

As in Bee? How do you get the audience of a decision maker's assistant who gives you the "Royal Push off"? First thing you need to remember is the needs of the Decision Maker and address his/her needs! Talking only about your needs will get you a quick path out their door. If you take the route of giving the Decision Maker reason to keep you engaged in the conversation, this will only enhance continuing of your audience. Remember, you need each other! The Royal Push off doesn't help either one of you. Being Busy is part of the journey. Other people's busy day is part of their need to stay employed; prove to them how adding you to their group will enable their life to not be so busy!

C

Calendar

You've always worked with a calendar. Now the test – find it. You have been diligent and organized. You were very busy attending all the meetings and conferences you were once required to attend. Why change that philosophy now? Have your calendar set up so that you will not miss an appointment, and neither be late nor too early for an appointment. Ten minutes is the rule of thumb if you plan to be early. You sure don't want to appear as a desperate candidate. Keeping your calendar updated and correct will minimize any angst that may occur with having a calendar error.

Call Center Jobs

Isn't this synonymous with Animal House? Are you a vivacious, Type A personality, and you have learned the art of multi-tasking? If you have answered, "Yes", to these questions, go for it! A position in a Call Center gives you a position to use your learned tasks. However, as the old adage goes, "If you can't stand the heat, get out of the kitchen", don't apply for a Call Center position! Energy personified is the key attribute you must have to be successful in a Call Center. If you have all the energy and spunk needed for this environment, great! Please stop and think about accepting a position in this environment if you need a calming environment with lots of time to do each task. In most cases, you will be timed and measured on each call you handle. You must also be that smiling voice that comes across the telephone lines to your customers.

Callbacks

Don't be surprised if an interviewer asks you to call them and they never call you back. It is all just part of their game. Either they don't know how to say, "no", or they are just plain rude. Just move on and forget about them. The consensus is that if you have not heard from the Hiring Manager in three to five days, and the Hiring Manager is not returning your e-mails and phone messages, it's good for you to move on to your next job opportunity. Remember years ago when people would say they were going to do something and you could take their word to the bank? Hate to break the news to 'ya, but those days are over! With the numbers being so high with applicants for the same positions that you want, it is an Employer's market. You could have met every criterion for the job listed; however, there might be another person out there who has more, more, more whatever, than you. Remember, your focus should be, "Why should the Hiring Manager HIRE ME?" If you were the Hiring Manager, would you HIRE YOU?

Calling

Contacts, connections, whomever. Do this a lot. You just never know who knows whom. The descriptive word for this is, "Networking". "Using" someone is not the message you want to convey! Call your contacts and first ask them how they are doing. Should they say that they are in bad times, offer to help by asking for their resume. If you come across something for them, let them know that it would be your pleasure to help them because you are also looking for a job. If, however, your contact states that life is great for them, things are going extremely well, and they are quite content with the way their paths are going. Then let them know how wonderful things are for you and you are excited about looking for your next exciting venture. You don't want to use this opportunity to tell your contact all the horrible specifics that have happened to you! You want to remain up beat, positive, and you do not want to rip apart your previous Company or Boss or co-workers. You also may use this opportunity to have an informational interview, just seeking information on various industries, or Organizations. The more you learn in the job search arena, the better equipped you will be to finding your next position and surprisingly so, your next position may just prove to be your happiest moment of working at tasks to your liking!

Calm

Desperation doesn't work. Your demeanor should appear to be calm on the outside. Try to control your insides, to the best of your ability. When conducting yourself with a calm manner, you will impact those around you with the same calmness. Remember, a chocolate bar is not a bad idea to fulfill a quick calming effect! Just make sure you know how to hide the zits unless you think they will help you look younger. Calm and Collective - Your nerves shot? Let's think of the worst thing that could happen==you don't get the position. The best thing that could happen is that you do get the job. By staying calm and collective you will put the interviewer at ease making the actual interview go so much easier. You are responsible for you and when you decide to take on that responsibility you will be proud of yourself.

Cars

Getting there, should it be clean? Keep your eyes on the road. Your interview studies should have been completed hours ago. Make sure you have a good battery, etc. Can you live in it? Who lives in it now? One never knows who will greet you as you park your car at your so very important interview. The cleanliness of your car will show them who you are. Also, a dusty dirty car will most likely leave its remnants on your wonderful interview dark blue or black suit.

Cattle Calls

Take a ticket please. Bring your own milk. You thought they only did these in tryouts for Broadway Shows? Wrong! They do them in Corporate America's Job Search World as well. Clues – you are given time windows for your interview such as 10:00 a.m. every Tuesday and Wednesday or you arrive and the reception area looks like an Obstetrician's waiting room. Companies that use this means usually have a high turn over. Also, the process for hiring may include a test and group meetings (no coffee and croissants). Maybe you'll get an individual meeting one-day with the hiring manager. Then if you get this job – watch out and keep looking for another.

Clarification

Ask what the prospective employer means when they give you feed back as to why you were not selected. Ask for an explanation why you weren't selected if all you got was a thanks no thanks. Okay – I got up and said good-bye and thank you and pressed the elevator button. What do you mean I didn't close at the end? The elevator door closed and I didn't get stuck.

Clothes

Good idea to wear some! Remember what you wore on your previous interviews. This is very important. If you wore a white shirt/blouse with a neutral color suit, let's say, black or navy, and it's still looking fresh and clean, you're ok! However, if you wore a unique outfit, let's say, aqua colored dress or suit, wear something else! The key here is to look clean, confident, and neutral. If your outfit is not clean, or it's too tight, that may be a cause for alarm. What you are wearing, at the time of your face-to-face Interview, should be the least of your concerns. You should have total control over this situation! Remember, looking fresh and clean on the outside, gives you more confidence on the inside! It's always better to dress up, rather than dress down, for this occasion. After you arrive at your appointed interview time, and you notice that the clothing style is Corporate Casual, and you are dressed 'Up', this is a good thing! Remember, they already work there and they know the dress code. You are looking for a job and you should be professionally dressed for your Interview.

Compensation

This is normally the money you as an employee receive from your employer for the job you performed. It is usually in the form of a salary (or wages) and also may include a bonus or commission if your job is in sales. However, be aware that some job ads may be misleading and unrealistic regarding the potential compensation. They could be just get rich scams asking for an investment on your part. These are usually get rich for them – not you.

Complacent

Has apathy set in? Turn your job search into a fun game if you start to feel this way. Now, you may ask, "HOW" do I make this job search into a fun game? Your mission is to win at the game of job search. Let's compare playing any game, whether it is a game of Chess, Scrabble, or Monopoly. Stay away from Park Place unless you are prepared to leave your keys in your car. While sitting at the game table, you have already learned that winning is lots more fun than losing. Therefore, you will turn your complacency into a winning scenario while you are playing the game of job search. Let's face it; there will always be a winner and a loser. Sometimes it's a wash, with dirt specs, all the players not winning, nor losing. Now it's your turn to focus on, "YES, I CAN" and, "YES, I WILL". You want to train your mind into thinking with a, "YES". When you present yourself either on a telephone interview or an in-person interview, presenting yourself with a positive reflection, is half the battle. Present yourself with a "PMA", Positive Mental Attitude. Bingo!

Computer

Make sure your computer is set to view foreign characters. This all may be foreign to you because you may need to use one in your job search so be prepared. Applying and searching has become very automated. Don't get stuck in this mode. Get out and meet people because networking in person will be very key to your job search success.

Confirmations

Affirm and re-affirm! It used to be that you would set an appointment and then confirm it one or two day's prior. In this microwave society don't be surprised if you feel that your confirmation fell into a hole. Show up anyway! Who knows you may add to your network if nothing else happens. Especially, if your interview is in a high-rise building. Elevators are great resources for networking. You have a real captive audience especially if you get stuck for a couple of hours.

Connections

Are you connected? Remember when you wanted to know about where you could find a good pizza? All it took was a phone call to a buddy who was into pizza and you got your answer to finding that perfect pizza. Being connected is just that simple! Whether being connected to finding a great pizza or finding that perfect position is right around the corner for you. Connecting to folks you already know, or folks that your folks know, is the best way to find whatever you are trying to find! Life, as you know, is give and take. Your phone call to a past buddy starts the process. You can call and say that you were thinking about that person and you were curious on how their life was going. They might say things like, "Life is great", or "Life is a bit difficult now". If things are great, you can update them on your life. Should things not be wonderful, you can be receptive, empathetic, and agree to help them as best as you can as you search for your next position. Being connected and staying connected is the best direction for you because it's people that create connections and connections help achieve your end result.

Continue

Don't quit, continue your quest! It might get somewhat disillusioning but don't let that happen. Think about all the times you began a diet, desired to quit smoking, lessen your drinking. All these things have never been easy but if you keep continuing your quest, it's all doable. Continue your job search activities and you will be successful.

Control

Pretend that you have your remote control in your pocket! Keep control during your interview. You are going to be tested in so many ways. Remember, you can control only what you can control. Should you find yourself in various situations, such as more than one person doing the interviewing and you feel as if you are being verbally attacked by all at once, you can be prepared with some catch phrases with humor. Ask them if you can move to the front of the class. As you take back the control, you will then be the Captain of your ship! Also, just because a question is asked, it's perfectly all right for you not to know the answer! We are not walking almanacs! We are not mentally tied into Yahoo!, BING! or Google! The answer to a question can be always used when you send your thank you letter. It would be a great follow-up with your added information and it gives you more to your incredible organizational skills. Remember, you don't know what you don't know, especially in a situation where there are more than one person interviewing. You may also find yourself in the middle of the interviewing group's egos. It would be to your advantage not to fall prey into them making you their attack victim. If you feel that the guns are out and you are being shot, defuse the situation. Once again, you will gain control and this is the best result for your controlling the interview process.

Cookies

Like to bake? Why not bake up some cookies and bring them to your local stores, for example, your local gas station. Ask the Proprietor if you can leave your batch on the counter and see if they sell. If they do sell, you have just given yourself a new job! Remember what you like/love to do and use that to begin your new career. Many job posting scams also like cookies. Watch out! If it looks too good it may be real good for them and not you.

Cover Letters, E-Mails

Cutting and pasting is a great tool. However, you sure do not want to send Mr. Jones a cover letter/e-mail addressed to Ms. Smith. Writing a cover letter enhances your chances for you to be setting the tone of why you are above the rest creating a competitive edge. By reading and understanding exactly what the job truly is, you have the advantage of addressing how you can take away the pain of the Hiring Manager by addressing your abilities for that specific job. A great Cover Letter expresses the purpose of your letter, addressing via bullets your abilities and experiences with what the Hiring Manager needs, that is in professional format, leaving lines between each paragraph, and creating a very easy format to read. Remember, most Hiring Managers do not like to read. They are being inundated with many Resumes and Cover Letters. Please remember to set your letter above your competition by having the reader want to read what you have submitted. After you have written your Cover Letter, take a step back and answer this question, "If I were the Hiring Manager, would I want to read this letter"? If you have written that perfect Cover Letter, your answer to that question will be, "Yes"!

Credit Checks

Many employers are conducting these prior to the selection process progressing. Be aware that what they do could impact your credit score. Ask them how they submit the credit request. They might try to use this as a method for acquiring your date of birth. Your date of birth should not be a requirement for this type of credit check.

D

Dates

Remember them. Whether it is Blind dates and every other kind of dates, keep your calendar up –to-date and correct. Now there are electronic dates. Appointments, made with your approval, make you responsible for showing up! DAH! "My dog ate my calendar, my clothes are still wet", these excuses for your foul-up won't win you friends and influence people! Any rudeness must not come from you! Should your appointment be cancelled or changed, that's ok. However, what is not ok is for you for set up an appointment and you can't make the date fail to let your Interviewer know ahead of time. How could the Interviewer conclude that you are the perfect candidate if you don't even acknowledge a change in the time and date with your previous set date? You certainly don't want to start a possible work relationship with the Hiring Manager not being able to trust your word with something like not showing up for your interview date.

Dealing With All This Stuff

Your cards have been dealt. OK, it could have been a better hand but now you have to play out what you were dealt. Your new challenge is having the willingness to deal with the realities of looking for a job; your feelings are all over the place. Give yourself a break! Of course, you are experiencing a roller coaster of feelings because you are losing or lost your job and/or angry and thus fearful. A concerned question you might have is will you be able to get a new job in a timely manner? If you begin to focus on the negative, mentally change your channel. You have control over your thoughts! Keep your positive thoughts and focus. If you need a better paying or just a paying job and are worried about not covering your bills. Burn them! (Please don't take this seriously, don't burn them, just wish you could!) Concerned what others might think of you. "Don't worry, be happy"! All your feelings are now on the table for you to deal and cope. Did you ever think that this is a great new time in your life? Dealing with the hope that your next position will give you a better day-to-day experience may just be what the Doctor ordered. (Wouldn't it be grand if he still made house calls?) This new challenge in your life may prove to be the best thing that could have ever happened to you. When was the last time you went to work without a knot in your stomach? Now is your time to deal with your emotions and you may now focus on your needs with regards to your next job.

Degree

What's your thermostat register? Two Year Degree, Four Year Degree, Master's Degree, Doctorate Degree, or continuing education from the plain old school of hard knocks? How far do you need to go to become qualified in your field? Is it good enough to have your experience in years or in Degree's? Only you can decide on what is good enough for you to gain the level of where you need and wish to go and to what level you need to be. Remember, once you earn your Degree, no matter what level you achieve, no one can ever take your piece of paper away, YOU earned it.

Direct Mail

What is this you may ask? Is this the opposite of "Indirect mail"? Yes you can send a quality letter/presentation on yourself via snail mail and it will arrive. Do your homework! When addressing your letter, ensure your letter is addressed to the correct person, not someone who used to work there years ago! Address your letter with knowledge of what the Company does, what history is behind the Company, and how you can fix their pain with the position you are seeking. Although Direct Mail has a low rate of success, Direct Mail has some rate of success! You will be unique because many take the easy electronic road. Remember, it will only take ONE JOB to ease your pain and to ease the pain of your perspective Employer who needs you!

Directions

Ask, use the web or get a reliable GPS – construction zones – one-way streets, are challenges when you are locating your Interview location. Be prepared! If need-be, take a dry run to your Interview destination. Remember, you are seeking employment, albeit, your hopeful next Employer needs the right person for their opened position, you are hoping that it will be you that is chosen. Should you arrive late, upset, sweaty, or totally unnerved, this would not be a great first-impression! Again, do your homework. Whether it is a dry run, printing out great directions, etc. you can mitigate your challenge of arriving at your location on time and without angst!

Discrimination

Do you fit the right mold for this open position? This company definitely prefers older workers. Consultant, Retirement Benefits HR Team is seeking a US Benefit Consultant. To be considered for this position, you must possess a BS or BA degree, 810 years exp in design and operation of benefits or 5 years exp + actuarial exp. Don't be disappointed if you don't get a call. This could be just the confirmation of their candidate pool.

Distance

Don't assume that you will be able to negotiate going into the office one day a week if the office is 60 miles from your home. Find out early on what are the hiring manager's thoughts. Your job search needs to accommodate your expectations.

DNA

Do not apply – minefields ahead – watch out. Let's look at the "hire'ees" position! Just because you have chosen to believe all the hype of a job ad, doesn't necessarily mean that what you are reading is above board. This, of course, is your course of action regarding how much you are willing to keep your ethics honorable. This is the harsh realty of the job search market. The job expectations today are that when a person is hired, they need no training, no guidance, and no training. Employers appear to expect the new hire to sit at a desk and do the job instantly. Welcome to our microwave world! Should you have 90% of the qualifications for a given job, unfortunately, that might not quite cut it for today's hiring manager. It has become an accepted practice today that in order to lower the stack of applications, for the requirements of a position, a candidate must have achieved a college degree, be a local resident, and have a pre-qualified number of years of experience. We will call these attributes, "DNA". Should you request the help of a Head Hunter, you will soon be quick to realize that your proven DNA is all the head hunter needs to find you your next position. The reason is because you actually do their job and they make the money by placing you by using your DNA to vie for the perfect job! The harsh reality hits hard when you want to begin in a totally new field and you have the DNA applicants beat you in the competition for the same viewing job you are seeking. When you are playing a new game, the object is to learn the rules as fast as possible and that will give you the added edge to be the ultimate winner. Someone is going to win at the game, why not let the winner be you?!

Do's & Don'ts

There are lots of these. Do show up on your interview. Do show up prepared. Do not wear cut offs. Do not show up late. When replaying your Interview in your mind, do focus on all the right things that you said. Don't beat yourself to a pulp for things that you should have and could have said! We all become the "Monday morning quarterback"! We know all the right answers after the fact. Instead of beating yourself up, do take the situation as another learning experience. "What have you learned from this situation" is more productive and more positive than if you choose to stay in the mode of telling yourself how you blew the Interview. Do give yourself credit for doing all the right things. Don't focus on things that you could have tweaked more, if given the chance. Just learn from them for your next interview. Remember, you will be writing a thank you note to your Interviewer. You can take this opportunity to focus on the positives, even after your Interview is over. Just remember that this position will be so much better with you in it.

Dressing For Interviews

Yes, it is a good idea to be dressed! Know your audience. Do your research and learn if Corporate Casual, dress down or dress up is the apparel of choice. It is usually better to dress up. Remember, you are the person seeking your next position. It is you who want to make a great first impression. You wouldn't want to wear something that will be a negative focal point for your Interviewer. If that tie, or blouse, or whatever, has a stain, wear something that doesn't have a stain. Visual appearance does matter. You yourself know that you have your own personal opinion of others when you first meet them. They, also, have their first opinions, when they meet you. Haven't you noticed that when you dress for success you not only feel better but also your shoulders stand up straighter and you walk with more confidence?

Duck

If it looks like a duck and feels like a duck it probably is one – move on don't worry. Most of us have a sixth sense. How many times have you yelled at yourself because you had a funny feeling that something was wrong but you chose not to acknowledge that feeling, only to kick yourself after you realized that your gut feeling was right? Here's where your sixth sense will come to be your advantage. While searching for your next job and a particular job interview leaves you with that feeling of caution, listen to yourself! If something feels wrong, than it is wrong. If you need to duck, do so! Remember, if the little hairs on the back of your neck rise, you know that you need to get out of this particular situation because it is not the right fit for you.

Duct Tape

Always keep some in your car. You just never know what might happen on your way to an interview. What would happen if your Glove Compartment lock breaks and you are not able to keep the compartment closed? That little light inside could cause a drain on your battery as you spend all day at round robin interviews. Not fun arriving at your car drained from interviewing facing a dead car battery.

Dueling For Jobs

Here's where fencing will come in handy! Some employers like to do group interviews just to see how the competitive traits come out. Keep your swords home. Humility works, arrogance does not work! Understand your audience. If you were they, would you want swords clanging? Should your competitors come out fighting, and you choose not to be combative, who do you think comes out the victor?? Remain the gentlewoman or gentleman that you are. Don't look to get the final laugh. You want to be offered the position; you don't need the final laugh. Stick to your plan. Remember why you are there and what you bring to the table. Remember how to address all your assets in doing the job that is being asked of you. Dueling is for those with egos. Keep your ego in your car!

E

Easy

Nothing in life is ever easy. Think back to an attribute that you wanted to acquire and remember how great it felt when you were successful in attaining that attribute? Your beginning search isn't easy but as each day passes you became closer and closer to your desired result. Remember keep that "PMA", Positive Mental Attitude. You will have productive uplifting days and disappointing days in your job search.

Ego

Keep it and leave it behind at the same time.

Damage to one will happen if you let those bed bugs get you. The lesson learned here should be, "leave your ego in your car". Be confident! You will be successful with your Interviewers. Turning around the need for your ego to be stroked will enable you to listen and observe. The focus is on your bringing the Interviewer in a non-defensive mode. This is a good thing! By showing that you are not out for the Interviewer's position, you will not become an immediate threat and it leaves the door open to a possible job position!

E-Mail Interviews

These interviews have replaced the traditional phone interview. They can be to your benefit. You can delete and change your responses prior to sending. Whereas on the phone, once the words come out of your mouth they are there. You can quickly hit mute but if your timing is off it won't work well at all. Remember to read your e-mail for grammatical errors. Spell Check helps spelling, Spell Check does not read for using the correct meaning of words. Your e-mail is in your total control. Before you push your, "Send" button, ensure that what you wrote has clarity, understanding, correct spelling, and is addressing your focus on what the purpose of your e-mail is meant to be addressing. Also remember, there will be no give and take in this interview and your personality and charisma will only be with your written word.

Emotions

Yes, you are allowed to be emotional at this time! Change, no matter what the change, is very difficult. Endings and beginnings are hard. Your emotions tag along with any change and may prove to be a major challenge. By allowing yourself a bit of breathing room, and by identifying your emotional dimensions, may prove to be a wonderful catharsis. By taking hold of your emotions that you can control and by identifying your feelings, you will then be able to label each emotion and deal with each emotion, possibly, one at a time. Emotions may have nothing at all to do with logic. However, you are the Captain of your Ship and you certainly have the ability to alter your course of travel. By understanding yourself and knowing that "YAHOO" You Always Have Other Options", you can change the direction in which you are headed and you just may surprise yourself when you realize that emotionally you just might be so much better when your original path changes and you wind up at a much better destination.

English

Can I just get the instructions for this application, profile test, etc. in English? I don't want to leave America. Globalization is very much part of our lives. As large as our world was, it is no longer big enough that we can't wrap our arms around it! Yes, English is the common language of many Countries and Business Sectors. However, English may not be English as the first learned language. In many instances, English may be the second, or even third language learned. With human dynamics being what it is, communication is extremely critical. Whether it be the written word or the verbal word, understanding each other is critical, especially in the world of Business. If you are searching for your next job, and you spend some time with researching the Company that is of interest to you, understand that where the Parent Company resides might possibly be in a Country where English is not readily spoken. It is up to you to blend into that ever-evolving Global Business World. Become more global in your thinking and your willingness to adapt to all communities will enable you to broaden your horizons.

Enthusiasm

Very important! Body language is very important! Your voice is very important. Remember, the Interviewer probably does not know you. Don't you value listening to a joyous voice? Don't you value meeting someone who exudes joy? Think about the fact that if you were Interviewing you, what would your evaluation be? Enthusiasm shows energy, and that's what you want to bring to your new audience of Hiring Managers.

Entry-Level Jobs

Are they for me? What does that really mean? If I start in the mailroom can I move from there? This is a very challenging question that needs to be addressed. If you are willing to change your career and you are willing to start at the bottom, just because you are willing to do that, does this Organization promote from within? Will there be opportunities for growth? What would your potential be as long as you are willing to learn and do? Once you understand the answer, and let's just say, "No", there are no potentials for promotion; would you want to begin your new career in such an Organization? By understanding the internal politics of this Organization it would save you much frustration and disappointment for you to put all your eggs in one basket and realize that you wasted your time if your mission was to grow from within and learned that will never happen. Ask the questions, get the answers. Knowledge is power!

Expectations

Amazing what happens when you plan that fabulous interview, dress for success, then OOPS! Everyone is running around in cut offs and t-shirts. Did you get off on the wrong floor? Or are you wrong for the floor? Sometimes we just can't write the script! It's very possible that what we think might happen, won't happen! You might be totally surprised that when you arrive at your allotted interview time, no one is available. Or, perhaps the opposite may happen. You arrive at your allotted time and instead of one interviewer, there are six people ready to interrogate you! If you train yourself to expect the unexpected, you will be ready for anything! "Great Expectations" was a great book but using that catch phrase within the confines of your job search may leave you with many experiences to share with your grandchildren!

Extra, Extra, Read All About It!

You have landed a position! Now is the time to write short notes to all those folks who were kind enough to help you. You never know when these folks can come into your life again.

F

Failure

Is when all else fails and you have lost your humor. Don't! For every challenge in your job search that you run across and do not feel successful with – laugh, learn and move on.

Faxing

Fax my application, resume - how do I find this prehistoric animal? FedEx KINKO's??

Feelings

This is more than a Barbra Streisand song! You are going to experience all kinds of feelings – ones you never thought you had. You will also find that interviewers will try to tap into your negative feelings by asking you pointed attack questions. Yes this is a test.

Film

Am I really going to be filmed? Who will provide my wardrobe? What? This is just my 2nd interview and not American Idol. So my role is to be the customer and you are the Sales Person? Take 1 – Roll the film. I'm ready to be a star. Oh no! Who is this woman who keeps coming into my office? Is she part of this? I wasn't told what her role was. Time to improvise! I will include her and see what happens. This just proves that I must be prepared for whatever comes my way and even if I wind up being filmed, I must be the best star ever!

Finding

Your dream job – does it exist? Yes, it does exist and you will find it before you land on that cumulus cloud.

Flexible Hours

What does this really mean?

The definition of Flexible Hours is the "Ability to work flexible hours". Hours for this position are Monday through Friday, 7:30 a.m. to 6:30 p.m. and Saturday, 7:30 a.m. to 1:30 p.m. Now if you are paying attention to these flex hours, what is this really saying? Flex hours have no flex at all! Your prospective Hiring Manager is really asking what?? "Are you available for any tour, any schedule, 24/7, depending on the Business Needs?" Say what? Remember, if you are agreeing to any and all hours at the time of the Interview; be honest with your reply after you understand what in the world they are asking of you. Should a weekend need arise and you have agreed to being flexible, saying, "NO", could possibly hurt your career choice. The lesson learned here would be, "Do what??? Say what???

Flirting

Yes this may take place as you are out in the world of interviewing and meeting new unknown people. This is the corporate world not the bar seen so deal with it as a professional. Also, don't fall into that trap yourself.

Fluent

When applying for a job that is requesting to be, "fluent", this is pretty serious business. If the request is being fluent in another language, they are serious. You can't pretend to be fluent in another language if you are not fluent. If you have all the applicable degrees but you are not fluent in what they are requesting, don't waste your time for applying to the job position. However, if you are being asked to be smoothly graceful and easy, that is something else. If your style is "fluent", and this is what is wanted, don't give up! Your mission is to find out what is being desired, fluent in another language, or fluent as being smooth; able to express yourself easily and articulately, you just might have a chance at this job position.

Flying

To an interview – use a Commercial Carrier, drink coffee only when wearing a brown color – turbulence happens when you least expect it.

Focus

Keep it! What do you do when you take a picture of someone or something? Isn't it true that you FOCUS? Simply by putting your attention on the subject at hand, you have created the perfect focal point. By the way, have you ever noticed that if you ask a busy person to do something, he/she actually gets it done? Why is that? The reason is a busy person holds the command on being able to focus on each task. The lesson learned here is that you must set yourself up for success! Have you designated a private area for you to 'work' at achieving success? Do you have enough light, enough workspace, enough quiet, to focus on your task at hand? These things are certainly within your control. You know "What" you want to achieve, finding a new work position, and now you need to focus on the "How" you will achieve finding a new work position. If you have designated your daily activities on job search, stick to that arrangement. By focusing on your desired end-result, you are half way to success!

Freedom

You've got it – enjoy it. Scream from the rooftops but don't fall off. How many times have you wished for the strength to change a bad situation? Perhaps now is the time to make your wishes become reality. Being FREE is a wonderful thing. You have the power to enjoy freedom and change your every day life into something empowering and positive. How many years has it been that you have wished to work at your passion? With the understanding that freedom is available and possible, with a few changes with your thinking and perhaps a few extra college classes, you have the freedom to move forward and enjoy your new world that's right around the corner. You are free, and now it's time for you to rally around this new thought and utilize your freedom to your advantage. We are not saying that this is an easy task, let's face it, nothing in life is easy, but by allowing yourself the freedom to change your limitations that you have given to yourself, you can now reach for the stars and capture the moon with the new freedom that you have given to yourself!

Friday

Oh No! Here comes another one and I ain't got no a job. Regroup and think about how you spent your week. Are you keeping a diary of all your new contacts, all your possible choices of positions, all your Interviews, Informational Interviews, and what you have learned this week? Just because it's Friday, it doesn't mean you haven't accomplished a lot with the current week. Every day you add more to what you have learned, with folks you have talked, what new Industries you researched, and you will see just how productive you actually were within this week. Every day you spend with Job Search, you will be that one step closer to finding your position.

Friends

Even their television show got cancelled! Where did they go? In times of change, true friends rise to the top. We all have friends that are very much part of our lives in good times only. During times of transition, those good-time Charlie's leave you adrift in the ocean, alone and cold. If you have friends that are negative and are always there to point out the bad, it's now time to weed out your address book. When you surround yourself with positive thinkers, you will become like them, positive! If any relationship is not reciprocal, it's truly not a relationship. There are basically two types of friends, the givers and the takers. In times of turmoil, the takers must take a back seat in your life. Should you find yourself with very few pencils to give, surround yourself with friends that are not looking for anything but your friendship. If this sounds like a difficult assignment, it's not difficult at all. It's your turn to take care of you and your true friends will certainly rise to the occasion.

Frog

Ribit, Ribit! What a horrible feeling to be on a phone interview or an in person interview and you have a "Frog" in your throat. Where did this term come from? As you are choking desperately hoping water will drop from the sky throw out a humorous comment – such as UGH! A frog is in my throat – Ribit! Ribit! Can I have some water or bugs? Here's where being prepared does wonders for 'ticklish' situations, such as this! Have some mints, cough drops, or something soothing for your throat, easily available, either in your pocket or pocket book! Dry throat is not unusual, especially when we are in a stressful situation. All you need do is simply say, "Excuse me"; I have a cough, and reach for a cough drop or sucking candy, that you already have on your person. You will be surprised how fast that lozenge will work and you can then begin talking, without having that frog in your throat! If at all possible, relax. Take a deep, cleansing breathe, suck on your lozenge and all will be ok! It is okay to ask for a glass of water if they don't offer it.

Fun

Have lots of it – run, bike, and play electronic games because job search can be so boring. Reward yourself with something you would consider fun. After job searching all week, perhaps you can give yourself a treat. This could be as simple as taking a walk, sitting and reading a book for pleasure, watching an old movie, or just doing nothing what so ever! Fun should be built into your week. You know what you would consider, "fun", and your reward of "fun" should be in your activities as part of life's adventures. Remember, "All work and no play makes Jack a dull boy"!

Funny Names

"What's in a name"? You will run across some hilarious names in your interviewing. Plan ahead how you will handle this. What happens if your phone rings and Mr. Bugsy Roach introduces himself or Ms. Fanny Smith? Learn where your mute is. What will you do when have to ask for them by name in your first in person interview? Rehearse? Rehearse? Rehearse?

G

Ganging Up

Remember that bully in school? Employers love to gang up on interviews so don't be surprised if you walk into what appears to be an auditorium for your interview. Hang on to the wall as you walk in; ask for water and most of all a chair. Remember, you aren't in control of the logistics for this Interview! The Hiring Manager and/or the Human Resource Manager are usually managing the interview. On some occasions, the Hiring Manager will tell you that a few people will be attending the interview. That will give you a heads-up on what to expect. However, not in all cases will you know that you will feel like you are against the firing wall and the Hiring Manager is leading his Team by saying, "Ready, Aim, Fire"! Your focus needs to be on directing your replies to the Group, keeping eye contact, and understanding that it is acceptable for you to ask if one person can ask one question at a time rather than have all the players direct many questions at you at one time. This is a great time for you to understand the human dynamics of the Company based on your gut feeling of the choice they have made on their interviewing style. It's also very important for you to give yourself the power to not only have the Hiring Manager want you, but you also need to feel that this job is what you want as well. Would you be comfortable in this environment should you be asked if you want the job? If you feel this is not a proper fit for you than it is all right for you to not accept the position. Use this as a learning lesson on how to handle yourself with this kind of interview.

Games Played

Internal posting, discrimination, etc. Valuable lessons have been shared through various chat rooms on the Web. When you find yourself in various situations about looking for a job with a start-up company, have all points of negotiation signed and sealed! Unfortunately, if you agree to work for a start-up company, and they say that 80% of the sales force must meet their target, think about the implications of such a declaration. Can you be responsible for others sense-of-urgency? Also, you should be privy to monthly reports that tell the story about what is sold, by whom, and when. If this information is not shared with the team, how can you know what your commissions are due you? Here's another point of, "Let the buyer beware"! Desperation causes many specifics to go unnoticed. However, if you are not receiving your money-based information, this should present a red flag to you immediately. This is just another sample of the Games that employers play to maximize your abilities and not match your dollars worth of pay.

Gap

This is not a commercial for your interview wardrobe! Your Chronological Resume is a flag to your interviewer reader. Over a year of not working becomes a challenge so a Creative Functional Resume may be the right choice. If you have been unemployed for less than a year, a Chronological Resume would be a better fit. Should you want to stick with a Chronological Resume, have you volunteered for the time spent of not having a paying position? Include that time to your advantage. Did you have a major health issue? Not a good thing to mention on your resume even if you are pursuing a career in Healthcare. How can you disclose your gap in an understandable way? Remember, on an interview; be prepared to discuss your employment gaps.

Glass Doors

What fun! You get off on the 30th floor and now are in a glass door maze. No one to be found! Do you have a phone number to call? Where's the bathroom? YUK! I drove 60 miles drinking water along the way. Help! This situation just proves that as you get directions and address of where your interview will be, be sure to ask all the questions as, "Where's the rest room"!

Goals

What are they? Think about them, live them then create a game around them. – There are a few ways to set goals. The first and foremost goals are YOUR goals. The second set of goals is perhaps your next employer's goals. Did you ever take the time to write out what your goals are? Perhaps this might be as good a time as ever. What are the top ten items that you can put on your "List of Goals"? As you job search, see if your goals match your prospective employer's goals. If those lists don't match, move on to other employers. Now, let's just say, for arguments sake, that you accept a job position as a sales person. There are a few ways a salesperson may get paid. If you can see yourself accepting a sales position with a declining draw model, (this is used to self-cleanse the sales ranks), you might want to realize that the financial benefit to force the employer is to force an employee to quit rather than to fire them and then unemployment benefits would not have to be paid. It is far better that the employer pays you a salary, albeit a minor salary, that way the employer is putting up some money and will be more willing to invest in having you succeed. Again, while approaching the job search, goals must be equally shared between employer and employee.

GOD

What do you think when you see this? Wrong – Try again! It is a posting for a job. It is an acronym for The Global head of Organizational Development. So as you read that "GOD" will be responsible for creating and executing the management development program and deliver measurable results, it could really be you.

Government Jobs

Where do I begin? Can I get one? What is this paying money for an application and instructions? Is this for real? No! Tests? What kind?

GPA

OH NO! How do I calculate it? I'm older than dirt and there has been GPA inflation since then – now what do I do?

Great Feeling

Keep it and enjoy your job search adventure. Feelings are a wonderful thing! GREAT feelings are the best yet! Certainly if we had a choice, it's better to feel great than feel bad. Who has control of how we feel? The answer, as you know, is, "YOU". It's so much better to feel great. Letting go bad feelings and replacing them with good feelings is a wonderful thing! Keeping that smile on the outside allows you to keep your smile on the inside. You can treat yourself to feeling great because it's perfectly all right to enjoy the great things that are around you, even enjoying the great weather days with the beauty all around. Controlling the things that you can control is the beginning of attaining the great feelings of every day occurrences.

Grey Hair

Should your hairdresser be the only one to know? Should you hide it or not is the question? Rude awakening is when you are at your dentist's office discussing your job search wows with the Dental Hygienist. She is 20 something looks at you and says at least you aren't going into an interview with grey hair you can't be that old. UGH! Only my hairdresser knows.

GUT

Feeling?? Use it! Stomach?? Hold it in!

Using your sixth sense will come in handy while searching for a job. How many times have you been in a situation when something didn't feel right, look right, or be right? When you listened to your gut feelings, weren't you happy that you did? If something just does not feel right, you need to act on that gut instinct. Your gut intuition is leading you in the correct direction. Don't turn that intuition off because you are receiving the best 'heads-up' possible.

H

Hair

Comb it! We live in a very visual and tactile society. Depending on what type of position you are craving, know your audience! Your hair should be clean, without any offending odors! Isn't it better to read this here than lose a chance at a great job simply because your hair wasn't combed?

Hand Shake

The handshake is commonly done upon meeting, parting, or completing an agreement. Do it! Its purpose is to convey trust, balance, and equality. If the interviewer puts their hand out, they want to shake your hand. They aren't asking for donations. When shaking the interviewer's hand, be careful not to give them the wrestler's grab. You could hurt them. On the other extreme, a limp handshake will leave them with an impression of you as an insecure weak person. Best is a firm handshake with eye contact.

Hanging

Hanging yourself feeling– don't let this get to you. Keep your pride. Here's where we must learn to forgive ourselves! We have blood in our veins, not ice cubes! We don't have the ability to write the script every time we speak to someone. Should we hang ourselves for saying something inappropriate or just plain stupid, it's ok to move on and learn from our mistakes. Communication is an art and learning how to speak to others takes some time and planning really helps. Perhaps having another person to role-play would be a good tool to learn how

NOT to hang yourself while deep in conversation. Practicing how to speak with a Hiring Manager would be a wonderful learning exercise. Remember, should you feel that you have hung yourself out to dry by saying something inappropriate, get back on target, just as if you were riding a horse and you fell down. Yes, you will get right back on the horse and proceed to once again to continue to speak. Remember this is not a movie where each word has been scripted. You are the author of your words and you will learn and grow from your mistakes and that just makes you a better person!

Headhunters

Recruiters, employment agencies, etc. – employer paid – retainer or contingency, applicant paid for what?

Help

Here's a great opportunity to ask your network friends questions regarding the company with whom you have an interview. Do your research! Use you Google attributes and learn about this Company. Do your homework and at your interview you will be so happy you put your time into the research. Help from advocates is a good thing if used properly.

Hiding Info

On web postings – now what do I do?
Do not assume anything! Technology has brought us many wonderful opportunities. Posting jobs on the web is more of a norm than an anomaly. However, 'Let the Buyer Beware". Hiding hidden costs are now more prevalent than ever before. Be an assertive and intelligent buyer. Know any and all charges that are being hidden and you won't find yourself in an exploitive situation. Remember, ads cost money. Find out if you have to pay for their ads. If a true job posting is

without cost, read further into the ad and don't sign up for anything without asking all the questions and research the hidden unknowns before you become victim to any scams.

Hidden Agenda

Yours or theirs? Past jobs, past lives, past just plain past. Now what do I do? I have a past.

Hiring Manager

What does that mean? How do I get to them? Network, Network, Network!

Homework

Remember when you came up with various scenarios', "the dog ate my homework"? You're in the big leagues now. You're not looking to get out of a doing a homework assignment. It is now time to ensure your homework is done, and done well. If you are looking into various Industries' for your next position, do your homework. Read, read, and read about that Industry. Here's where you will learn truly that knowledge is power! As you research industries, you will be able to see what goals match your goals. Does the company you are researching have the same vision that you have? Are their ethics a model of your ethics? There is absolutely no excuse for you not learning as much as you can about your future employer. Doing your homework now will not only prepare you for their "test", but it will ensure you of knowing what you are talking about when you sit face-to-face and talk with meaning and direction. Doing your homework upfront can save you much time in finding the job of your dreams!

Hotel interviews

Spot check, make sure you know who is there. Your customer or work associate may be attending an event as you sit waiting for your interviewer from a competitor.

How

Do I begin? You already have begun your job search by reading this book! How many times have you heard, "Knowledge is Power?" Your power will come when you read and understand the variances of the Art of the Job Search!

HR

How do I get out of this loop? Is there a decision maker somewhere? Hello! Where are you?

I

Identity Theft

Yes this can happen to you as you innocently submit your information on what you think is a valid job posting. We are in a WWW of job search and the rules have not all been written yet.

In Demand

When you are on that upward trend, don't stop. The momentum will build with your positive attitude. A much needed attitude in your "Interview Hell". Even if this is as a result of your interviews with those who will hire people who can just breathe. Just use this as a confidence builder as you laugh at such an opportunity.

Informational Meetings

Giving and taking. A famous quote from Shakespeare, "Neither a borrower nor a lender be", is not exactly what is meant while speaking about Informational Meetings! Knowledge is power! How many times have you heard that said? Every day that you learn something new is a great day. When you have an Informational Meeting, this puts you in a more advantageous position. When thinking about a subject, your brain thinks with one vantage point. When you speak with others, they share their vantage point and that gives you an edge of looking at a situation with more dimensional sides. Having an open mind and listening to others speak helps you gain information that perhaps you would not have had the opportunity to learn at all. By becoming a sponge for all new information leaves you with more options and gives you more power than you thought you even had. If you thought about turning your passion into a real job, speak to those folks who are already in that job. Ask, learn, and understand their viewpoint of how they turned their passion into a paying position. You actually might just surprise yourself on all the added knowledge you will accumulate simply by utilizing, "Informational Meetings"!

Inside Sales

"What's in a sale? A sale by any name will still smell as sweet"! Wrong, inside sales just might be a fancy term for Call Center Sales. If you like to make a call every two minutes eight hours per day then this is perfect for you. Do your homework regarding Call Center Sales positions. If you would like to work in that environment, prepare yourself before your interview for this type of position. These positions are usually very low in hourly pay and the tasks are very rigid and repetitive. If you were re-joining the work force after years of a hiatus, perhaps this would be a good springboard for you. However, should you accept such a position, and that will leave you without time to continue your job search for a more rewarding career; perhaps you need to think about what your priorities are and work from that need. Just remember to understand what you are searching for within your scope of what you need and want. Don't sell yourself short! True you won't have all that windshield time driving around in your car. Instead you will have a manager watching over you with a whip.

Interview

In a supply closet. Don't be surprised or thrown off if your interview surroundings aren't the typical office, conference room. Some interviewers use strange interview places to keep their control. What would you do if you were escorted into a walk-in supply closet for your interview? Leave your claustrophobia home! Keep your cool and your humor. What would you do if you were meeting an interviewer at the airport? Sure you'd probably assume the interview would take place at the airport coffee shop. Don't be surprised if it is in the Baggage area and you are being interviewed as you show your capabilities of lifting 50 pound suitcases while answering questions about your life's ambitions.

Interviewing

Maintain your control; make sure it is you behind the answers. Did you ever leave a conversation and wonder how you said what you said?

Inventions

Voicemail – what a wonderful thing – not. ☺☺ Love it! Hate it! Avoid it! Use it! Abuse it! All of the above are all part of this job search game!

J

Jerks

They will be here, there and everywhere, especially on the other side of your interview desk. You just might find yourself in a position where your Interviewer is part of the "1-800-NO CLUE Club! Just because the Hiring Manager has his/her Title, doesn't necessarily mean they are astute and personable. Adjust and maintain! Do the best you can! Be yourself! You can shine, even under those circumstances. You are applying for a position because this Hiring Manager has a need for someone to fix his/her pain. This is your opportunity to show how you can be the savior of this Hiring Manager by listening and communicating the many benefits of your becoming part of this Organization.

Job Ads

"Reading is Fundamental", was an advertisement that stressed the importance of reading. Yes, reading IS Fundamental, but what about writing? Wouldn't you agree that writing is fundamental as well? As you spend some time reading the job ads, whether they are on the Web, in the Newspapers, or whatever the source, did you ever think that the written descriptions of the specific open job functions could be funny? If taken literally, some of the jobs need to be filled by super robots. There are so many requirements for one job that a working human would not be able to fulfill the requested requirements and can prove to be extremely overwhelming. In some cases, clearly there are typos and it was poor proof reading on the part of the writer. For example, $0.00 per hour is the hourly rate that the Company wants to pay! How would the payroll clerk handle paying FICA if your salary were nothing??? Aren't you screaming to work for nothing?!! Of course NOT! Would you send your resume in response to this job ad?

- Pay rate: $0.0/hr - $25.0/hr
- JOB DESCRIPTION:
- Ability to type 55 WPM
- Ability to communicate effectively (oral and written)
- Physical requirements- performs work in a sitting position up to 8 hours, required to bend, stoop, and must be mobile to support attorneys and staff in other areas of the Law Department.
- Provides secretarial support to 3-4 attorneys (1 Sr. Attorney & 2 Jr. Attorney - Attorneys are in Environmental and Corp section.
- Proofreads documents for accuracy
- Maintains pleadings, chronological and reading files
- Places, answers and refers phone calls

What do you think about requirements that are not explained? What does this Job Ad mean?

- I am looking for a VP of sales and marketing for a compelling Storage start-up. The role would be based in Boston. Storage focused candidates only!

The writer asks for functions without definitions of what their needs truly are. How can anyone be expected to become the writer's mind reader? As you are forming your opinion of the Company that is putting out the job opening, and as you read the mistakes, don't you already form an opinion of the Company that doesn't take pride in what their ads are saying? Would you want to work for a Company that doesn't stress pride in how they present their Company? You have already put forth a negative feeling before you even start filling out your application! Yes, writing is FUNDAMENTAL just as Reading is Fundamental! Some blind job ads may list their preferred companies in the background requirements. What does this mean? Can I assume this ad isn't my employer if they are listed on the preferred list? If you want to stay employed while looking, it is best to avoid responding to such ads.

Job Applications

Electronic or PDF – what is you pleasure?

How do you apply for your jobs? Have you ever thought what is the best way to answer a job posting? Remember, you have the power of the pen and the way you present yourself in bold lettering is what your possible future employer will see. Hard copy may be the preferred method for your potential employer. If so, remember spell check and the delete key do not exist. You will be typically asked standard questions on your application. They will include requests for dates of employment, job title, job duties, supervisor contact information, reason you left and your salary data. They can ask for the dates you attended College but not the dates for High School and probably will.

Job Boards

There are niche Job Boards, Generic Job Boards and everything in between. Many companies prefer to only utilize their corporate websites. Work from Home, Become a Private Investigator, etc. Don't be surprised if you apply to a job selling job postings to then be directed to your matches on their job posting website. Remember, everyone out there wants to earn a buck and using your name will help them, and possibly you! The Job Board is out there to help. And you thought your microwave was quick and handy! The anytime, anywhere communications have reached every facet of our lives. Now it's even in job search. The other positive note here is that it is an instant advisement of what's available as far as your job hunt continues. You can set yourself up for job match notifications in an anytime anywhere means. Just make sure you have a good signal so you can call and not sound as if you are deep sea diving in your job search.

Joking While Looking

Don't lose your humor. You will find some very funny things during your job search adventures. Please enjoy them. When all else fails don't lose your humor. One of the best stress reducers is our ability to laugh. Having, or creating, a sense of humor is not only appreciated by others but also will give you a three-dimensional personality. Also please remember your audience! A joke with some folks may prove to be hysterical. However, that same joke, with not the right audience, can prove to be disastrous. Keep your sense of humor, enjoy the path along the way, and you will find that when you reach your final destination you will have a smile on your face as well as having a smile in your heart!

Joining Professional Chat Groups

You do need these. They will be your lifelines.

Joy

Don't be afraid to feel it and express it after you land that job of your dreams. You deserve it. You sure worked hard for it. You are now on your honeymoon in the Bahamas, the sun is shining and the clear blue water is sparkling. You are in the Arrival Phase of "The Morale Curve", filled with enthusiasm, fantasy, and motivation. Enjoy this wonderful moment. Listening to your favorite song, going to the park on a perfect day, having enough money to pay your bills, all these things are part of your joy.

Judging & Judges

There are many in this job search process. You never quite know who could be the strong influencers. So be nice to that guy in the elevator. He could be the son of the person you just interviewed with.

Jungle

Job search is one so go find that tiger in yourself.

Justify

You will be asked to justify your deserving of the position you that you are being interviewed. Here's where your homework will come in handy. This question should come as natural as breathing. Your justification of this position should be as easy as water off a duck's back. Remember, do your homework BEFORE your interview.

K

Kindness
Where did this go? Lots of promises.

Know-It-All
Humility goes a long way. Don't be a know-it-all; just know enough to land you the job!

Knowledge
1-800 NO-CLUE – how do I get past these folks? Or should I move on and forget them?

Know Thy Self
Who me?? Remember when life was not so full of choices? It was possible to get either vanilla or chocolate when deciding on what flavor ice cream to buy. Then, the 31 flavors came to be. Now more choices than ever were available and what to choose became an issue. Let's face it, you know what you like! Just because there are many choices available, you know you and you know what pleases you. What happens when you begin your job search? If you know you, whom of course, you do know you, why would you apply for a job position that deals only with computer work 100% of the time when you are truly a people person? Keep in mind that you know who and what you like. As long as you keep in your mind that you know yourself, have enough respect for your self to keep to your plan and

utilize your strengths and weaknesses to determine what you need to seek and achieve because, "To thine own self be true"!

L

Landing On Your Feet

Treat every day as a new bright day and learn from the yesterdays. Falling down will be easier to handle when you realize that all you need to do is pick yourself up, dust yourself off, and land on your feet!

Language

Learn one prior to your interview. English would be a good choice if your interview were in the US. Some job posting specify the language preferences and requirements, i.e. fluent in English.

Late Hours

They don't care so why should you. Don't be surprised if your cell phone rings at 7:30 p.m. on a Friday evening from someone who found your resume on one of the Job Boards.

Legalities

Date of Birth, citizenships, etc. – when can this info be requested?

Lessons Learned

None yet – Don't worry your cycle has not completed yet

Likeability Factor

How do I get one? Where do I apply? Ever meet someone where their personality is worse than nails on a chalkboard? You can't change others, but you can change how you interact with them! Your mission is to have your Interviewing Manager like you. If you feel like a Dentist pulling teeth, change your demeanor. If you feel that there would be no way that you can win this Hiring Manager over, rethink about this position! Likeability factor is real. The basic interview embraces not only if you are capable of doing the actual job, and if you are a fit with the others who are part of the Organization.

Listen

Listening is one of the most important aspects of your Job Search. Hearing what others say increases your knowledge of what people need. Should you find yourself in a situation where you are speaking too much, your impact on others will decrease. The Hiring Manager usually wants to be the leader of the Interview. Should you decide not to listen, your points will be lessened. Practice your listening skills. Please make sure to wear your hearing aid if you need one. You will engage the Hiring Manager in a mutual discussion. Answer the questions that are being asked. You can do that when you are in the listening stage. Listen to the warning messages. They are words such as - we will call you don't call us and we have so many candidates and you are just one.

Listings

They are everywhere. Often they are not what the employer is truly looking for.

Looks

Yes you might get some strange looks as in up and down from your interviewer. Ignore them. Just realize that you most likely won't be hired by that person. Do you really care?

Love It Or Leave It

Yes, you need and want a job. Remember, every day can prove to be a long day if you don't like what you are doing. Being that you are starting over, why not start over with a position you will like? Do some mental homework and think about what you want to do and then go after that. Wouldn't it be to your advantage to work at something you would enjoy?

Low-Level Job Surprises In Your Interview

You know you are in the wrong place when they ask you to take a typing test and you have a PHD in Physics.

Luck In An Interview, On The Job Boards

Just like going to Las Vegas if you have no one in your network.

M

Magic

Abbra Cadabra and poof, there's your perfect job! Many days in your job search you will feel that all is needed is magic not luck and of course not skills to get your dream come true job.

Manage

Now that you are in your Job Search, learning to manage your time is paramount. Should your neighbors, friends, relatives, know that you are home, do not become their errand person. Your time is now dedicated to Job Search. You can't spend your time doing the errands for everyone. Would those folks expect you to perform errands if you were employed? Managing your time and focusing on what you need is absolutely required for you to become successful with your Job Search. Solicit referrals from these folks.

Many

Many job ads, many resumes, many interviews many disappointments, many opportunities – we hope.

Marketing

Yourself & sandwich signs will work if you are selling food. When selling yourself be proud and get off the streets.

Math Tests

Some companies require these tests for College graduates – HUH! Why?

Microwave Minutes

Your moment of glory has arrived you now have a real in person interview. Now what? How do you condense 25 years in one hour? Remember, the reason why you are having an interview. It's not to provide a job for you. The purpose is for you to take the pain away from the Hiring Manager because there is a function that is not being done currently and it has been determined that this function needs a person to fulfill the void. You would be a positive candidate if you address how you can add value to this opening because of what you have previously been successful doing and focus on your Interviewer and his/her needs, there's your microwave minutes giving you the biggest bang for your buck! Please remember, this is NOT about you, it's about your Hiring Manager being pleased that you not only can perform the tasks, but why you are the best candidate possible.

Mirroring For A Job

You may find this as your interview process. Just don't break it.

Miserable

Just plain miserable – why?? I combed my hair and brushed my teeth today. What an event that was! Whatever happened to that tooth I left for the fairy? I mean the fairy who gave me a quarter or more under my pillow not the ????

Missing Info

Make sure you have all of your ducks in a row – they will ask for everything.

Mistakes

Pencils have erasers because humans make mistakes! If you are human, you will make mistakes. Adjust and maintain! There will be many mistakes during your Job Search journey. Don't worry be happy. Use them as a learning tool. Mistakes make the best 'new products'! As you write a note on your sticky post it note remember that a 3M employee who was working on glue solutions created this in error. Voila a real masterpiece. Think about peanut butter hitting the chocolate. Think about so many improved products that became famous due to a mistake or two! It's ok for you to have mistakes because the new and improved version of you will be just that, new and improved! We are all so much smarter after we know all the facts! How many times have you played, "Monday morning quarterback"? We always know the answers after the game is played. Could we also agree that no matter how well we perform an analysis on a given contemplation, are we also right with our end results? Let's take Jeff, for example. Jeff had a well paying position, working in his field, and was not at all being considered to one of those employees to be downsized. However, Jeff just wasn't that content and he decided to venture forward and seek a 'better' paying position. Well, he did just that. After accepting another position because the Hiring Manager professed many promises, only to learn the harsh reality that the truth was not told regarding the new position and Jeff absolutely hated the stress, the unrealistic sales numbers that were part of his required sales, and Jeff is now left with a major decision, does he stay because he's worried about what his resume will look like or does he listen to his heart and leave after speaking with the Hiring Manager telling why he needs to leave. A mistake is a mistake when we choose not to learn from it. In this case, was Jeff's decision to leave his current job to seek a better position; the answer is "No". How could Jeff know that his Hiring Manager was not telling the truth? How can Jeff put this situation in his mental diary and make this a learning lesson in life? Anytime we have the ability to learn from a mistake, that's a good thing! We become smarter when we make mistakes and learn what we may do to prevent the mistake from happening again. Did Jeff receive his job position tasks and expectations in writing? Perhaps that would be one thing that could prevent this from happening to Jeff ever again. Think back to when you were in school, learning. Can you not agree that most of what you learned was because you made mistakes and then you needed to learn the correct answers? If we choose to look at mistakes as learning tools, perhaps beating ourselves up won't need to be as bloody! Let's take a mistake as a learning experience, move on, and prevent the same mistake revisiting your life!

Money

Sure is nice to have some! If you are currently working and receiving a paycheck, please start really saving as much as possible. If you have been already let go and you are pursuing another position, why not work part time at something else to carry you over with your bills? It is possible to work part time and still look for a full time position. Remember that "PMA"! Positive Mental Attitude!

Morphing

As in job opportunities? Headhunters may use this term to squirm out of the last opportunity they wasted your time on before they vanished. Now they need you again – they think sooooooooooooo. How can a job as a Sales Account Executive morph into an Operations Executive

who is accountable for a budget of 25 million or more? DAH! You are right! The headhunter really needs referrals and not you for this. It's almost as though the Headhunters want to fit you, a square peg, into a round hole! It's not a fit, but it's the way the Headhunter earns his/her living! Perhaps it is with this thought that your first allegiance should be to yourself, not your Headhunter. You are the most important piece of this puzzle. You will be beginning a new job with high hopes only to realize the job that you have accepted is not the job you thought you would be doing. The lesson learned here is:
Beware of the Morphing scenarios!

Motivation

Ever listen to the kids' channel? Song to verse is part of entertainment. For example, a song was written with the verse talking about how parts of the body fit together. If you ask a kid to sing the song, even though the words are difficult, the kid can recite what he/she has heard. Why? By sharing a great tune and putting the words to song enhances learning. Most kids love music, especially with a good beat. They will listen to the song and then learn the lyrics. Now, you are asking, "What does this have to do with Motivation"? Everything! You can present all the right tools for people; you can provide the nicest desk, the nicest pen, and the nicest anything. The one thing that can't be given is Motivation. Either a person is motivated or not. Ever think about what motivates you? Perhaps this would be the perfect time for you to have an introspective on what motivates you. Is it money? Is it time? Is it low mileage to work? Is it no commute time at all where virtual office may suit you? By understanding what your drive is, it will be somewhat easier to figure out what and where you want to be, either in your personal life or your work life.

Murphy's Law

We've all heard about that famous guy, Murphy. So why does he still have his job? Too many times haven't you wished that you never heard about him? Isn't it true that you have never voluntarily invited Mr. Murphy to your home? In the most stressful situations, don't you find that Murphy rears his ugly head? Knowing about Murphy is one thing; it's now time for you to plan on his visit! "Everything that can go wrong, will go wrong", states Mr. Murphy. What control can you take from knowing this? PLENTY! Controlling the little things make big things controllable. If you are wearing a white shirt/blouse and you spill something on it, which is usually the case, have an extra shirt/blouse in your car, briefcase, or whatever. You never know when that extra shirt might come in handy. Have gas in your car! Don't begin a trip to an interview with your gas tank reading "empty' unless that is what your brain is reading! PLANNING life's necessities will help keep Mr. Murphy away from you! Your mission is to keep Mr. Murphy away from you at all times!

N

Name

Yes, your name! Do a web search on yourself. You will find it very interesting to see what shows up. Many employers use this as a tool to investigate you. If you have a name like John Smith they probably won't bother with this route. If you are set up on networking sites, it will be much easier for them to learn a lot about you without searching too much.

Needs

You have needs and so does your potential employer. Express them! Your potential employer will for sure. Clear the air early regarding the issues of your employment. Don't wait 6 months after you are on the job.

Negotiate

Are you reading this and saying, "I can't negotiate"? Negotiation is built into your life, day in and day out. Don't you 'negotiate' a turn while driving? Don't you 'negotiate' what you will eat for breakfast? Don't you 'negotiate' what television show you watch? Life is one negotiation after another. It's now time to play with the big kids! NO ONE can read your mind! Regarding Job Search, it is up to you to determine what you want, what you are willing to accept, and what you willing to settle for while negotiating a job offer. Only YOU may determine what your needs are. When you determine what your needs are, you can then negotiate the other major things which of course include your salary. Should you need better benefits or more vacation than is being offered, this is a negotiation item. Don't feel that you have to sell yourself short. You are in the driver's seat now. If you are too easy to accept the terms of the initial offer, you could possibly lower your negotiation position. Remember, you have already gone through many phases of the process. You had your initial Interview, possibly the second Interview, and through the elimination of the others that were in the running for this position, they chose YOU! Why me? Why me? I'm so excited. Knowing this, you are in a great position for negotiations. The one rule here would be don't begin negotiating until you firmly receive a definite Job offer. True negotiations happen after you are offered the position. True you would just love to jump up and down as Martin Short did in his job interview skit on "Saturday Night Live" and just say Yes and not have to get into negotiating what you really need, want and deserve. This phase can be real awkward because you're negotiating about you and not a car.

Networking

Electronically or emotionally? What is networking? How do I find it? Do I need it? How do I connect with it? Of course, my Net is working. I use Cable at home and Wi-Fi when on the road. What do you use for your Net? Feeling lost in space! Known network? What is that? Unknown network? What is that? What happens if my known network becomes unknown? Business Networking sites such as LinkedIn are more geared towards job search. Social Networking sites such as Facebook might help you locate your old high school sweetheart. Then there are sites such as Twitter where you can tell the world how you feel. One never knows who may be following you. Think of it as one of those old party phone calls whereby your whole town is listening in. Networking, in general, is one of the best things you can do to help find your next position. Think of all the folks that you used to work with, the folks that you met at parties, your school buddies, Tell everyone you can that you are looking for a position and have your networking associates help you in your search. After all, you are their networking buddies as well as perhaps some day you will be in a position to help them.

Nonsense Job Ads

How to detect them. Some stick out like a sore thumb. Others are subtle. Unfortunately, some nonsense job ads are nothing but absolute scams. Once a job ad asks you for money, your charge account information, or anything to do with you paying them for anything, this is a pure scam. Nonsense job ads offer people aid in their moments of pure panic. Desperation should never come through as you deal with others regarding job search. Don't succumb to the trickery that the scam artists perfected. Remember, if something is too good to be true, the reality is that it is too good to be true. Listen to yourself. Your inner self speaks and sometimes we choose not to listen. Now is the time to listen! How many times have you said that you should have listened to your inner self and you didn't? Learn from your previous mistakes. Listen to your inner self and you will know the right choice. Those nonsense job ads are not worth your time and expertise! Move on!

Notice

As in job resignation or looking at one. Don't get so excited about your new job that you neglect to treat your present employer with respect. Make sure whatever you have to say is to your employer first and not to your networking community.

Offer

"Show me the money"! Yes you will get to see these so don't get discouraged. Now the fun begins. Is the offer what you expected? Does it cover in writing everything that was discussed? Make sure everything you're offered is put in writing. Don't be afraid to ask. You have been selected and you just never know how things may change. What would you do if all you have is verbal and your boss left the company 2 weeks after you started?

Old

Are we talking 'chronological' old? You may feel this if you are over 20, especially as you are trying to keep your many wonderful years of work history to 2 pages on a resume. Chronological numbers defines what? Did you work your way through your education while working full time? Did you have a family in between paying positions? What does age really constitute? How old is old? How young is young? Chronological age can prove to either be an asset or a liability, depending on your outlook on life! You are who you are, all of you. You have gotten to the part of your life where you bring all you have learned throughout the years. If you allow yourself to own your assets and down play your limitations, you have now become your own marketer! With your head held high as you search for your ideal job position, you should consider how lucky a hiring manager will be if they choose you to be part of their team. If you can answer the question, "If you were the Hiring Manager, would you hire you", if your answer is, "Yes", then don't allow chronological data stifle your job search.

Overqualified

But I'm only 23 and I don't even have a college degree. How can I be overqualified? Overqualified has various definitions. Could it be that you are asking for too much money? Do you have more certifications than your Hiring Manager? Are you holding more degrees than the Hiring Manager's Manager? "Overqualified" may have many reasons that are totally unspoken. Usually, when the term, "Overqualified" is given to you as the reason you are not a candidate, as hard as it might be for you to understand, it has nothing to do with you. The behind the scenes realities will not be shared with you at all. It is possible, however, to defuse this objection of being over qualified by stating upfront that you are looking to begin with a new Industry where you would enjoy starting from the bottom and where you would mitigate your over qualifications. Addressing this would tell the Hiring Manager that you are not looking for a huge salary at all. If that's the way you truly feel, that's would not be a bad position to take. During the interview the overqualified concerns may be hinted at and not actually expressed. You might be asked why would you be interested in a job like this after all the successes you have had in your career. In addition, using the term, "overqualified", could be scapegoat terminology that they just don't like you!

Overtime

Don't be surprised if you spend many hours at your job of job search finding a job. Your time is worth a lot so rather than spending many hours in overtime, begin a regime of beginning with a regular schedule that makes sense for you. If you used to work, let's say, from 9 to 5, that should be the hours you put in to find your next position.

How do you schedule your Dentist's appointment? How do you schedule your Doctor's appointment? Remember, time is money
Don't let this job search urgency overwhelm and overload you and your life. Having a work life balance is a good thing even in job search.

Overwhelmed

How do you eat an elephant? Give up? The answer is, "One bite at a time"! Michael Angelo painted the Sistine Chapel. Don't you think he painted one frame at a time and not the entire ceiling at one time? Yes, of course he did! Getting overwhelmed is an easy accomplishment. However, this is one accomplishment you don't want to own! Break down your activities. Write things down. This would be the best time to bone up on your organizational skills. Remember, eat the elephant one bite at a time! Control the things that are within your scope. Allowing yourself to become overwhelmed takes much energy away. Better to accomplish something then not to accomplish anything!

Oxymoron

What do they mean when you see captions like this on job ads?

- Industrial Refrigeration Sales - Hot Job
- Hiring – New and Used Sales People

When you see statements, that contradict each other, it's time to revisit the job ad!

P

Paper

What is this? Where do I get it? Do they use it? Yes! Paper thank you letters sent via snail mail can definitely leave a lasting impression.

Passion

Oh sheets! Passionate people do passionate jobs - inside and outside of the house. The first step towards this would be to sit in a quiet setting and think about what you would love to do if money were no object. Obscenities not accepted here. You are looking for a job and not stimulation. Well-------?? Upon waking up in the morning, or evening, or what ever be the case, what would it take to keep your passion alive? After deciding on what your passion is, then think/dream about how you could parlay your passion into a paid position. Here's a list of some of the Industry's that hire passionate people. (On Second thought, any industry that brings you passion can be a passionate industry!!!)

People

We need them and they need us – maybe? Barbra Streisand sang it so well. Do you remember one of the first lines from the song? "People, people who need people, are the luckiest people in the world"! Yes, indeed, even with today's technology, it's people behind the scenes. It's a mutual admiration society! With Job Search, people are the movers and shakers. With all the job postings on the web, the most beneficial, productive ways of finding your next position is through people! The need for the Hiring Manager is to find the best possible applicant for his/her position. Your need is for the Hiring Manager to hire you! The more people that you let into your life, the better chance you have in finding that perfect position.

Personalities

There are many flavors behind the interview doors. 80% of the folks hired are based on this intangible. Once upon a time there was a Class entitled, "How To Deal With Difficult People"! The take-away from that experience was you can't change others, but you can change the way YOU deal with them. You have the power to change your way when dealing with difficult folks! With so many folks having different experiences, coming from different homelands, and having different educations levels, of course there will be many personalities out there! In fact, do you remember the movie, "Sybil"? How many personalities did she have? While, at times, it can be very challenging to deal with various personalities, you can be the victor by changing your method of dealing with them. For example, if you know the person you need to deal with is a talker, let him/her talk! Should a person only want to get to the bottom line first, do just that. Get to the bottom line first!! Pick up on other's traits, so turn it and make it work to your advantage.

Phone Interviews

It used to be that your interviews were in person. Don't be surprised if you are asked to have a phone interview with someone who is 2 miles away. Phone interviews can be to your advantage. Turn off your call waiting and keep your phone's battery charged. If you have a dog, don't schedule the interview when the mailman is due to arrive. Barking can really be distracting when you are trying to sell yourself. Also, if you live in an environment with shared walls prepare your neighbors that you need their support to not play drums when you are scheduled for your phone interview. If you can't make these adjustments prior to the phone interview then go to the library with your cell phone and hope that they don't all have head colds and coughs there.

Phone Numbers

Make sure you don't have a typo in your contact numbers. I sent out so many resumes and replies to ads to then only discover there was a typo in my phone number. Now what do I do? Here's a great opportunity for you to resend your resume with the correct reach numbers and you can state in your new cover letter that, "Whoops, an incorrect reach number was pre-printed" and here's the correct reach numbers. Remember, what pencils have at the other end of the writing point, an eraser! Errors are made all the time. It takes a wise person to address and own the mistake and continue forging ahead! Mistakes happen! Humility goes a long way with people. Better to be humble than to be arrogant!

Phony

Not genuine! These folks stick out like a sore thumb. As they tell you how they manage their office they give you that big phony wink. They have no clue about the legalities, etc. Do your best not to over power your interviewer? Again, here's where humility becomes a part of your persona.

Plan B

Always have one! "YAHOO" means You Always Have Other Options! You might feel as though you are boxed into a corner but in reality you are not. You are only boxed in if you allow yourself to be in this position. Bearing your current employment situation as it is today, regroup. Take a piece of paper and brainstorm your thoughts of what else can you do at this time? Don't be negative as you begin writing. Remember, brainstorming is just that, jotting down various thoughts without any negative comments. Have you ever given great thought regarding what it would be if you had your choice to begin another career? Do you own a home? Would moving be a viable option? Would you be willing to relocate? Could you go back to school and achieve another Certification? These are all thought provoking questions that you can think through as you prepare your brainstorming list. Plan B, as well as You Always Have Other Options are very doable if you only give yourself a chance!

Politics

Not this again! The hiring manager will often find a way to hire someone from his or her known network even if that candidate never meets the 80/20 rule. Don't be discouraged. Make sure you tap into your known networks for your next job opportunity.

Pool

As in water – deep under?? As in lots of candidates – deep under ?? Swimming in with ——so many others?? Is this the methodology for you?

Predicting

The outcome – don't predict! Sometimes we can't write the script! Predictions are fun when you open up your fortune cookie! How many times have you mentally written the script, only to find out that your prediction did not match up to the actual ending? With any situation, the unknown is still the unknown. We become "Monday morning quarterbacks". We know the winner of the game after the game was played. With a prediction, any prediction, it is not the end-all and be-all. You may think you blew an interview and then you receive a call asking you to come in for a second interview! Of course, the opposite may happen. You might be sure that you have all the qualifications for a position, you predict you will get that position, and you find out that you did not come in first as the best applicant. Put your energy into focusing on what you can do. Learn from the experience and think how you might do it different the next time. Don't think negative that this time your perceived mistake was viewed as a mistake.

Presentations

Plan on these being part of the interview process. You may get asked to give a presentation as if you are selling a product such as a stapler and the only product is you. Perhaps you may be asked to create a presentation that you have never presented. Be aware of odd requests if you are interviewing with a competitor.

Prey

Think as in hawks not as in praying in Church. Ask the question? Have you become their prey? During a networking conversation - is it time to beware of your becoming prey for those who have ulterior motives? If you send your resume to prey hunters, it could put you in a position that is vulnerable to distressing emotions. Be aware of who you are addressing, whether it be in writing, speaking or via networking events. Keep your eyes wide open. Don't become prey for anyone looking to take advantage of you. They are lurking everywhere.

Professionalism

Say what??? Thank you and please are real nice words to remember. Also, words such as sweetie and honey are not appropriate even if you forget the interviewers name and need filler. Just leave some air space in your sentence instead. No not a lot of hot air space.

Q

Qualifications

What are yours and theirs? Is there a match? There is a mutual need. The Hiring Manager needs a function to be performed. You are looking for a position. Your key question, to yourself, should be, "Are you qualified to do the job". If you are qualified for the open position, that's a great start in acquiring this position. However, if you are definitely NOT qualified, move on to another open job. It is a good time to state here that jobs are sometimes not even known to the Hiring Manager. After you have researched the Company, and you have a great idea on how the Company can improve their business, you can talk about your qualifications to do a job that was not even advertised! If you have gotten an interview with the Hiring Manager and you are not qualified for the job being presented, you will give a very bad impression for wasting the Hiring Manager's time.

Qualities

Do you know yours? One of the first tasks for you to address is what are your strengths as well as what are your weaknesses. Most likely these two points will be brought up when you begin your networking, your informational interviews, as well as an interviews. You know your qualities, however, did you ever think about writing them down and documenting your strengths and weaknesses? When you think about your weaknesses, how can you turn them into strength? For example, if you say that you are weak in taking a little extra time before signing a document, is that really a weakness? Wouldn't you agree that showing that you want to use your knowledge before you sign on any dotted line, you have shown a weakness that is really a strength? Be prepared with your qualities. If you don't know yourself, how would you expect a Hiring Manager to know you?

Queries

What does this mean on job search sites? It means someone looked at your resume. You have no idea who or how valid they are. If they are not valid you will probably hear from them because they need to sell you something. Don't get discouraged when it seems as if that appears to be the only contacts you get. Times will change as you build your network and fine tune the presentation of yourself.

Quickly

You speak to a recruiter and they inform you that they want to fill the position quickly. It is a new position and they found your resume on a Job Search Board. Well actually, there are two positions – one Junior and one Senior. Then they inform you that you might fit in either one. Don't jump up and down with glee just yet. Be aware that they might have a friend they want to hire and need to justify that they have interviewed other candidates.

R

Rambling

You will find yourself doing this during the interview. Put out that big red stop sign quickly. When creating your resume and cover letters just remember to stick to the point or you will get that pointed finger sending you out the door. If they begin yawning or doodling during your interview answers, this could be a heads up that you are rambling and boring.

Reality

It hasn't been lost by this experience – you can find it again. One of the reality shows, "Survivor", has been a huge hit! Why? You see it all in a weekly hourly television show. You see how the universal theme, "Man's inhumanity to Man", is captured. You see ethics thrown out the window when it comes to staying in the game. Have you given it much thought of how much you are willing to alter your code of honor with searching for a job? It is up to you to decide how much you are willing to negotiate your beliefs. Who you are as a person means a great deal when you are put in a situation where it is very easy to skirt the truth, alter the truth, or not even tell the truth. The strong suggestion here is to be true to yourself and have your word be your bond. Should you tell an untruth about what your reality is and has been, it is very possible to come back and bite you. Your reality is just that, truth and honor, if that's what you choose. You can be successful by achieving your next position using your reality and expressing who you are as a person and sharing your background and experiences with those you come in contact.

Reading

Keep current; be prepared for this to be an interview question. What would you answer if the interviewer said what is the most inspirational book you ever read? What would happen if you said "The Bible" or "The Teachings of Buddha" or "The Teachings of Kabala" versus "Re-imagine" by Tom Peters? We are not saying that in order to find your next job position you have to be a Rhodes Scholar. What we are suggesting is that "Reading is Fundamental"! Keeping up-to-date with the news, new discoveries, major world strategies, and the like, will make you more of a rounded person where you can talk about various topics, not just in your area of expertise but an all around motivated person. Think about the people in your life that you enjoy being around, talking with, and learning from them. This is the type of person you just might choose to be, if you are already not there!

Red Flags

Look for them! Not an amusement park – just your gut feeling. Should something not feel right, it's not right. Give yourself enough respect that you know when the hairs on the back of your head stand up and they are standing up for a reason. How many times have you found yourself in a position that you knew something was amiss and you chose not to listen to your inner workings? After the situation ends, you kick yourself because you didn't listen to yourself. Give yourself credit for being astute in knowing when something doesn't feel right. How many times have you been asked for your opinion from others and you gave them great advice? It's now your turn to listen to yourself and give yourself the greatest advice as well. If you see a Red Flag, or feel a Red Flag, act on that and have courage to know what you know is right. Believe it or not, you're the best ally to have! Don't let this job search game make you feel so desperate that you neglect to read your true gut feelings. Otherwise, you may take a job that is truly a mismatch for you and then find yourself back in the world of job search.

Referrals

These are great if all the stars are lined up in the sky. All the books say that this is the only way to get a job. Okay? What happens if your referral loses their job midstream as you are negotiating the job offer you received from their referral Company? A referral is wonderful, but it's not the panacea to a job search. Getting your foot in the door is a major milestone, however, your referral may get you into the door, but you need to stay away from the revolving door! Be sure to do your homework. Research the referral Company. Find out who are their competitors. Check their credentials, for example, are they in good standing with the Better Business Bureau? Again, a referral is great as long as you do your homework to maximize your introduction.

References

Contact them first, spell their names correctly. It is best to have a prepared list of references that know you personally and a list that know you professionally. Identify where they fit in your past job experiences. Most of all make sure they know who you are and will be saying good things about you.

Regret Letters

Learn to love these letters / e-mails because it is better than never hearing back from that company you spent hours talking to. You will get everything from e-mails sent from an @invalidemail.com address to one mailed via snail mail. The snail mail ones may come looking like they were typed on recycled used paper or the mail smells like perfume. Just remember that it is better to be informed no matter how smelly it is.

Rehearsing

Study the answers to potential questions that may be asked of you in an interview. Look in the mirror and make sure you have a positive approach and attitude in your responses. "Paper or Plastic", "Is that to eat here or to go?" "Did you say, 'Super-Size'?" are all wonderful lines to learn when all else fails! If you live in a metropolitan area and there is a commuter train, think of all those folks who travel back and forth. Where are they going? They are going to work! There are too many folks utilizing the commuter trains every day and they have to be going somewhere. Do not give up hope! YOU WILL FIND ANOTHER JOB. Remember, it only takes one job that will leave you with a 'feel-good' attitude. Rehearsing to the positive thoughts will be much more beneficial to you and your emotional state rather than becoming Chicken Little, the sky is falling! You can take your job search and truly put it towards rehearsing for a play. You have the determination to write your script and learn your script and practice your script. You have more power than you think you do because you know what you are seeking. You have the drive and determination to be successful. It is now time to begin your rehearsing of how you want your end-result to finish. Rehearse the positive and you will find that you will actually live up to your expectations!

Reinvent Yourself

What does this mean? Why can't I just be me? I know what I have to offer so why is everyone asking me to be someone else? This term appears to only exist if you have been – right sized, downsized – not if you are still employed sized while in your job search. That is okay! You will be better off as you move to your fun, new self.

Rejection

Expect it. Learn from it and move on. You only thought people who are in sales get rejection. Guess what! You are in sales now. Your product is you. When you do accept the job of your dreams go have fun with these folks who never returned your calls. Call them and leave a message that you wish them the best of luck in their candidate search because you are delighted to inform them that you have accepted an offer with another company.

Requirements

Do you ever scratch your head when you read job requirements? Here's one to ponder: Requires canvassing existing businesses, offering to save them money by lowering their merchant service rates. Go after new businesses that need to process credit cards. One-on-one training. Some outside sales experience preferred, but will train. Felonies ok. Straight commission to start. Here's another for a temporary full-time job:

- Minimum Job Qualifications Required:
- Physical exam (325 lbs. weight limit)
- Valid driver's license
- Non-negligent driving record
- Test qualify on varied employment tests
- Ability to hear test and set tones
- Lift up to 150 lbs.
- Able to perceive differences in wire and cable color.

Or one like this that clearly identifies that the foods and beverages we consume are filled with nasty chemicals:

- Candidates must possess 5+ years proven experience in technical sales and have a background in processing, chemical, beverage, or food industries.
- A degree in chemical or mechanical engineering is a plus.
- Major account experience, skills in addressing both plant and corporate level needs, and knowledge in fluid dynamics and/or turbo machinery is required.

Relocation

Benefits, are there any? Do I care? Of course you care! Have you ever thought of moving, especially for another job? If you have the opportunity, and desire, to relocate, start a-new, and begin again, relocation would be a great advantage! If you take a piece of paper, draw a line down the middle, with the two columns you have, write, "Pro", and "Con". Under each column, write all the things that would be applicable. At the end of the page, you will be able to see where the biggest column lies and you can then work from that vantage point. Relocation just might be the right answer for you, as well as your family and friends. While in your job search, leave no stone unturned. There are options. Remember the word, "YAHOO": You Always Have Other Options!

Restaurant Interviews

Don't wear white … and don't order anything that would tend to wind up on your clothes or face! Any food substance that you wind up wearing should be not ordered! Items like spaghetti with red sauce, spinach, or messy finger food should be left on the menu and not ordered for your plate! If spinach winds up in your teeth, how do you think you would feel when you look in the mirror after your interview is over? When in doubt, leave it out!

Resumes

Short, long, electronic, paper – thin, thick, white, gray? Too many choices and what's the definitive definition of the perfect Resume? For every person being asked their opinion about your Resume, you will have that many answers! A Resume is a direct mail piece. The first few seconds is what you have to connect the reader with your Resume. A generic Resume is as good as 'one size fits all'. Is it true that one size fits all? Of course not! Your resume could be the best of the best but if it doesn't answer the needs of your intended reader, then does it matter how great your resume is? The very first step of having a great Resume is to know your audience. If you would role play and pretend you are the Hiring Manager and you have received your Resume, would you feel that the piece of paper addresses what you are looking for in regards to your open position? If your answer is, "No", now is the time to prepare your Resume with the end result in mind of having a Hiring Manager read your Resume? If you have many years experience in a particular Industry and you are looking to change your Industry, address your Resume with information that proves you have the abilities to do the current job you want. If you have managed a large group of people, changing industries would most likely still have a large group of people to manage. Remember, a Resume states who you are and what you have done. Word smithing is good thing because you want your Resume to stand out from the rest of the folks submitting to the same job position. Your mission is to have your Resume in the 'keep' pile. Address your Resume to the needs of the reader and you will be on your way to achieving your perfect Resume!

Ringer

As in washing machines or interviews? They will probably say I want to set up an interview with you, myself, and maybe one other. Don't be surprised if you are put in a room of five attacking you with questions and staring at you as if you have a boogie hanging out of your nose. Practice and plan for these potential scenarios. Perhaps having a tissue with you wouldn't be a bad thing!

Rip Off's

Misled, deceived, beguiled, betrayed, befoolled, chicaned, flimflammed, fooled, gulled, hoaxed, hoodwinked, hornswoggled, tricked, deluded, double-crossed, or otherwise RIPOFF Now where do you go? You go to your own intelligence. You listen to yourself. You realize that if something is too good to be true then it truly is too good to be true. You can only be ripped-off if you are not the wise consumer. Read all the small print and you will not be coerced into something that you are uncomfortable doing.

Risks

Creating a resume with your background versus what you think they are looking for. Whatever you do, taking a risk doesn't include not telling the truth. No risk is worth taking if you get caught in a lie!

Rolodex

If you are looking for a sales job you may see this in the body of the job ad. Don't be surprised if during your interview you are asked to provide names of contacts from your customer base. Think about how you want to approach this. They really mean it and will probably write down the customer contact names that you provide. Will they hire you? What is their purpose for this? These are questions you should address.

Rules

Do we need any? What are they now? Remember when you played games as a child? Remember how the rules sometimes changed? With Job Search, sometimes the rules won't include, "Do-Over's"! Here's where being polite, courteous, and humble should be very much part of your Rules and Regulations! Words like, "thank-you", "thank-you", and "thank-you" should be part of your demeanor. Humility works so much better than arrogance.

S

School Of Hard Knocks

Have you graduated from this School? It seems that most of us graduated with high honors! "Experience is the best teacher" has been used as an old adage. Unfortunately, going through the School of Hard Knocks with having various experiences to ponder, perhaps graduating from the School of Hard Knocks can help you understand the pitfalls of what may happen when not prepared for various situations. The lesson learned here is, "Be Prepared"! Do your homework! Learn all you can about Industries that entice you. Learn about what jobs make up the Industries that interest you. Read, learn, research, and talk to folks that already hold those positions. You don't have to attend the "School of Hard Knocks" to gain all the knowledge of moving forward with your Job Search. Look for the answers to your questions and you will avoid attending this school!

Screen

As in phone interview or patio for mosquitoes??

Search Engines

What does this mean? I search and search and ??? Today's technology has opened the gap for finding almost everything with a touch of a few keystrokes. Whether using "Yahoo", "Google", or others, you are now able to research and learn merely sitting at your home computer leaving the days of having to go to the Library or having to own the latest version of a full set of an Encyclopedia's is not high on your priority list to purchase. The one thing that you should keep in mind is that you are not the only one researching available jobs. Many others are using the same technique of using Search Engines as their primary source of hunting for their next job. Don't put most of your energy and time by only using Search Engines! The lesson learned here is that broadening your known network will increase your job prospects. By using a Search Engine, you will be putting yourself in an "unknown network". Balance your job search time with utilizing not only the various Search Engines, but by creating a strong known network. You will also find there are search engines for tying together all of the entire numerous job posting sites. They usually charge a fee for this luxury into the "unknown network".

Seasoned

What are they talking about? Me, a seasoned turkey, seasons as in Spring, Summer, Fall, or Winter? Or a descriptive count for my very many or lack of years of experience? Depending on how you are using "seasoned", seasoned can be a positive word or a negative word. Be careful when using this because the reader can take exception to what this word is really being meant. Should I use seasoned or something else like older than dirt or extensive experience to explain myself on my resume summary, cover letters and other correspondence?

Secretaries

Also known as gatekeepers. You may run across secretaries instead of voicemail when you contact the hiring manager. Be prepared as to how you will deal with them. Gatekeepers can be real rude at times. Also, on the opposite side of that coin, Secretaries can be your best allies. Keep in mind that you need them and as you present yourself in a non-condescending fashion, and you treat them with total respect, you just might surprise yourself when the Secretary facilities your meeting with the Hiring Manager! Remember, communication is an art. Also, your priorities are not necessarily others priorities! That in itself is a great lesson to be learned. In fact, we'll say it again, "Your priority is not another's priority". Being courteous and warm does not always get you what you want, but certainly, by being curt and nasty, that won't certainly gain you friends and influence people! Secretaries usually know everything so it is in your best interest to treat them with an extra smile in your voice. This just might be your ticket to getting what you want!

Selling Short

Don't! You know your short fallings, Interviewers don't! Pointing out your short fallings and dwelling on them would not be in your best interest. Ever notice when someone tells you, especially woman, (!), that your dress is nice? Your comments, might be, "Oh, I got this on sale"! Ever notice how we are never worth retail? Or, you will point out a rip or tear somewhere on your person! Or you are told it is snowing down south? Enough focusing on your frailties! Positive statements exude positive behavior and that's what is needed at the time of your Interview. Your Interviewer is looking for a person to fulfill a job position that is strong, and knowledgeable. Turn your weak points into strong points. Should you not be a strong quick thinker, you can say that when you make a decision it is the best decision because you focused on all the points and rather than waste time and money with a quick answer, your answers bring home the best pathways for the right solution to the open issue. You might also add that you have been commended, many times over, for your diligence to researching and understand the ramifications of a tough decision and you came out the winner!

Serendipity

Yes, you too can experience Serendipity! Should you decide on opening up your windows of opportunity, allowing laughter to enter your soul, and take the worry out of your tomorrows, the expecting the unexpected will become part of your everyday happenings? So many of us have prepared ourselves for the due-diligence of life and then a fork enters our path and we aren't sure of which way to turn. Have you ever thought of what might have been if you took the other path instead? Now is your turn to accept the serendipity. Good things happen to good people. You are good people. It's now your turn to enjoy the changes, embrace the new possibilities, and as you have heard so many times before, turn that frown upside down!

Settling

In job search hell – take me take me! What 50 cents per day I am yours. After months and months of rejection, you will be so very tempted. Don't! You will regret it. Hang in there your best opportunity is just around the corner.

Side Jobs

One good side job is looking down and sideways as you walk. You will be amazed how many dollars and coins you will find. Have you ever thought about having two, three, or more, part-time positions? You are multi-faceted. Perhaps you can have a part time position working a few hours, a day, or per week, doing something that you would love. You can then get a part time position that pays some real dollars. Even though it wouldn't be your true passion, you could endure a few hours a day, a week, for the money, and you will know that your full time days/weeks would not be overcome by activities you don't love. You don't have to hold on to what you think is the norm for the working world. You are now your Master of your Ship.

You steer, you choose where your destination will be. Can you appreciate all the new power that you have given to yourself?

Signs

I created a sandwich sign and am standing on the corner begging for a job. I am wearing Business Dress so why is everyone spitting on me as if I am a homeless bum? I networked and tried everything – time to advertise myself to the world. The sign that you are putting forth is the sign that you are looking for a job. No, you are not a bum and no one should be spitting on you!

Silence

Is it golden? No news is good news? No news is no news? Now what? I have tried to communicate with no response. None! NATDA! No response after 3 interrogating interviews. How intimidating! Boy do I want to give them a piece of my mind. Feeling like a one night stand! Now what?

Skills

Yes, you have skills! Don't take for granted the things that come naturally to you. That is what makes you unique. Think about all of the skills you have. Even ones you haven't used in ages. You just never know what will give you that extra leading edge over the other candidates. Some recruiters believe that technical skills over the recent three years are only appropriate to emphasize. That used to apply for programmers. However, Y2K changed things. What did the resumes of all those beach bums retired COBOL programmers look like?

Small World

More than the exhibit at Disney World!

If you haven't heard the, "Six Degrees of Separation Theory", many times this statement has been proven right. The reality is that we do live in a small world! If you don't know someone, your cousin's cousin on your Mother's side, twice removed, knows that person! With technology today, our world has gotten smaller. We have access to the world with a point and click on our computers. Things that used to be a challenge to comprehend, no longer leaves such a challenge. There are very few gaps, if any, that if you really want to close the gap in your world of knowledge, you certainly can. Living today has indeed made our world smaller and the sky is your limit to what you wish to achieve. The option becomes yours. You need to decide on how you can manage your philosophy of acknowledging your world has indeed become 'small' and you can certainly be a 'big' player! If he looks like someone's father, he may be someone's father. Maybe he is the father of the HR person who you spoke to and had zero chemistry with.

SOAR

Not as in flying. This is an acronym you may often hear when discussing behavioral interviews. SOAR stands for Situation, Obstacle, Action, and Results. Be prepared to discuss these items about your jobs when interviewing.

Sorting

All this nonsense stuff – do I care? How do I do it? Here's where the lesson learned from a cable television program, "Clean Sweep" could help! When you are overwhelmed with stuff, sorting out what you need verses what you have saved, may prove to be a wonderful catharsis. Sorting your thoughts can be simplified by sorting out your environment. If your visual perceptive is being taken over by 'stuff', perhaps now is the best time for you to do your own, "Clean Sweep".

Look at what you are saving and hoarding. Are these things memories that you will lose if you don't have the items with you? The best way to begin your sort is to say to yourself, "If I didn't look at this stuff for over a year, then I don't need it". Please be cognizant of papers that you are required to keep for whatever the legality states. Your checkbook-cancelled checks are not needed if they are dated twenty years ago! When you begin this mental sort and you transfer the mental thoughts to the actual physical sorts, when this process is over you will be cleansed of your baggage and you will be able to walk into the room of doom into a room of serenity. It's your choice, "To sort or not to sort, that is your question"!

Speaking

The How To books on job search say let the interviewer do most of the speaking. That is just fine if it is you and the interviewer. What if you are in a conference room being attacked by questions from 4 or 5 people? How do you fit questions into your answers to get them all speaking? Don't forget to speak when they ask you a question.

Spell Check

Watch out! Names look funny when they are corrected. You will find many humorous job postings as well because we all now rely on Spell Heck. OOPS! Meant Spell Check. The lesson learned here is that spell check does not check for meaning. You can spell everything correctly but the meaning of what you are writing is not what you wanted to state at all! Proof reading is still a very necessary task and if you happen to have someone close at hand, perhaps having another person read what you have written will be very helpful because another person's editing can come in very handy! Should you not have someone close, walk away from what you have written and then come back and then re-read your script. With a fresh eye, you will be able to check for grammar and understanding with regard to your written words. Better to take a few moments to proof read your letter than to send it off only to find later that you made a big faux pas. "Better to be safe than sorry"!!!

Spirit

Keep it! Don't let the tedious activities of Job Search take it away. If you need to have a pity party because you are not happy with your current job situation, allow yourself 30 minutes a day to feel bad for yourself! After that time frame, gain back your control and keep your spirits high! Think about the type of people you choose to be around. Of course being with a black cloud over your head leaves you without too many friends! Therefore, your friends would appreciate your black cloud changing into perhaps a blue sky! Your spirit is you, you own it. Why not give yourself a feeling of well being rather than choosing a morbid spirit. After a while, you will even start feeling and believing your spirit roar because it's the best feeling to be filled with hope and there is no better than feeling hopeful! Keep your spirit high and you will see the difference with your behavior!

Stick To Your Knitting

Not with needles unless you have a dispute with your employer. What we mean is know your strengths and weaknesses and stick with them. Frank Perdue, chicken Guru, did just that…he stuck to what he knows best! Diversification sometimes just doesn't work. If you stick to your strongest strengths, how could you possibly lose? It could prove to be that by sticking with your strength success will find you! If you have strength, you would probably agree that your strength is also your passion. When you are passionate about what we believe, how could you fail? Soar with your passion and stick to your knitting!

Stimulus

Money, money everywhere – why can't we (get a job) play the game? This is getting very frustrating. We (I) need some of this stimulus money that is being spoken about continually. The other issue is when we do receive our stimulus check, where do we put the money? Do we pay a bill, buy a new suit for interviewing purposes, or just squander it, perhaps save it? What a position to be in!

Stood Up

What do I do now? They said they would call at X time on X day. I sat by the phone waiting and no ringy dingy. I called my phone company's customer service to make sure that I had not accidentally selectively blocked those numbers, an outage occurred, etc.

Study

Understand all you can about the company with whom you are interviewing. Be prepared with questions that show that you have done your homework. Don't ask them questions such as how to spell the company's name or what is their product.

Squares

Which one do you fit in? What you don't know? We are having a collision of generations in the workplace. Why people are living longer, working longer, etc. Baby Boomers: (Born from 1946-1964) represent the largest population ever born in the U.S. Their large number created a competitive nature for jobs and opportunities. They typically grew up in the suburbs, had educational opportunities above their parents, and saw lots of consumer products hit the marketplace. Generation X: Many members of the Generation X emerged into the workplace during the 1990s expansion and this is the smallest generation in terms of numbers. They had a distinct competitive advantage in choice jobs 'they wanted.' The technological revolution exacerbated their successes, as they are techno savvy unlike their Boomer competitors. Rather than paying their dues for a number of years as previous generations did, they were able to demand that organizations adapt to their ways of doing things creating disbelief from the Traditionalist/Boomers. The Gen X'ers have made the work place a better system for all of us by demanding flex hours, telecommuting, etc. Gen X'ers grew up as a skeptical group due to fractured family systems, violence in the news, AIDS, drugs, child molesters and downsizings. Generation X'ers detest micro-management in the work environment and want constant feedback on how they are performing. Gen Y/ Millennial Generation: This techno-savvy, multi-tasking generation has had access to cell phones, personal pagers, and computers most of their life. They have, for the most part, led privileged lives traveling more than previous generations to worldwide areas, owning the best in technology. Futurists predict they will change jobs 7-10 times and even change careers 2 or 3 times. They were also taught to question parents/teachers and the status quo. Where's HAL?

Successes

Every day you will have successes. Remember them! Celebrate them! You need to focus on them – they are your friends. Even if it was that your gut was right about a jerk you interviewed with. Or a scam ad you decided was real scum.

Sucks

Yes it does! Don't let it get you down and out. Pretend this is movie and the script is being written for you. Understand that the interviewers hate this process as well. They have their jobs to do and are probably not real sure how they can figure out who is the right candidate for the job. They may want to slat to the 80% chemistry factor but need to feel the warm fuzzies that you also have the 20% can do the job factor.

Surprises

Don't be surprised! Anything can happen and change. So if you are preparing for an interview that you are so excited about to then find out they already extended an offer to someone, but liked your background so wanted to talk to you just in case. Or, if they had a plan for the interview to be just informational because they like your background, but not for their job. Or that exciting Customer Service job with travel becomes a high-pressured call center job during your interview.

T

Telecommuting

What does this really mean? In the car a lot visiting customers, working from home or what. Find this out early on – especially if you live 150 miles from the office. There are many definitions of the word, "telecommute". Your understanding of this word and a perspective Hiring Manager's perspective of this word may not mean the same thing. Your best bet would be to understand the Hiring Manger's definition of this word. If you are being told that this is a telecommuting job, you might think you may be able to work from your desk at home. In some cases, this definition may mean that you will be driving to your clients and you can do your paper work from your desk at home. You may also find out that 75% of your time will be driving. To save a lot of angst regarding your possible telecommuting position, find out what this word means to your hiring employer before you sign on any dotted line!

Telephone Tag

Create a new board game that works with the buildings you acquire during Monopoly.

Called office phone left message – 2 points, called cell phone left message – 3 points, received a voicemail – 10 points. Stop! Enough! Just send an e-mail when all else fails and ask when will be a convenient time to connect. Better yet offer a few choices of dates and times.

Tenacious

You will need to be in the Job Search world. Regroup your thinking. Remember your past experiences. Think back to when something was very important to you and you were determined not to give up until you reached your destination. It could have been *wanting to buy a big-ticket item and you needed to save until you finally reached the dollar amount. It certainly didn't come easy but you were determined to save until you could have what you wanted and needed. Now is the time to be just as determined to find your next position. Hold on to your desires and make it happen by building a realistic plan of action and following it through until success hits. Tenacity is a good motivator and it's not a bad word when used with the meaning of staying focused on your end result.

Terms & Conditions

Whose Terms and whose Conditions?? While reading the job ads, before you sign your name to anything, PLEASE read the T&C's! The free job availabilities may prove that it will cost you real dollars for each point and click. "Let the buyer beware", which would be you in this case. Remember, if something appears to be too good to be true, then it is too good to be true and it will cost you financially later on.

Tests

Oh no my personality is failing. Is there a course I can take that will help me pass? How does this impact my GPA? What tests?

- **LIMRA** preparation – get out your insurance policies, banking, brokerage accounts, list of who's who and your first-born.
- **FAST**- Do you have a pass or fail personality? This will not be appropriately named if the desktop computer is in an

entertainment hutch with spot lighting on the computer screen and the only place for the keyboard is on your lap.

- **SPQ** Gold – Bring your birth certificate – Red, yellow green – originally created in 1980. Okay new test – which generation created the SPQ Gold and which generation was it created for?
- **Corporate Insight AVA** – this one will be your future after you are hired
- **Concord**???!!!

Why do so many of the companies using these tests have such high turnover? That is because most people answer the tests to the get the job and not as to how they feel or operate. Some keys: You want to make a lot of money; you don't like sitting home reading a book; you like parties and interaction with other people; you are willing to work until the work is done; you are a self starter. Keep those in mind and you should do well on a sales test. On an insurance test, always have 250,000-500,000 in life insurance and if it is whole life you get extra points. (You can't sell what you don't have, thought pool)

Drug Testing – BYO, what are these employers checking? Will they see if I have any medically age related problems, am I pregnant, etc.? Some items sold in Health Stores may cause testing challenges such as DHEA. Buyer beware! How do you pass one of these tests?

Thank You

After your interviews, don't forget to write a thank you note to the person or persons who interviewed you. A personalized thank you note goes a long way!

Thank You Notes

Electronic or snail mail, when to do one – when you are feeling thankful and inspired. No matter what form you use, a thank you note is in clear order of the day. Not only does a thank you note bring you back to the Hiring Manager's desk, but also you will now have the opportunity to bring something else that was omitted from your interview. If you were talking about a topic and you didn't mention that you had experience with that, you certainly can mention that in a succinct manner. It's also a great time to bring up a correction that you would like to clarify. Regardless of what you still have to say, even if it's nothing, thanking the person for their time is absolutely the correct thing to do, whether it is a snail-mail thank you or an electronic thank you. You don't want to look back and be remorseful if you didn't take the initiative to send your thanks for the opportunity to meet with this person. Do the proper and right thing with regard to thank you notes!

Time

Choose it – what is it? Are you a morning person, etc.? Where did it go? How do I respond to a request that asks for a 30-minute phone interview time slot? Be On Time - The one major rule of the day is always be punctual. Do you like to wait for people? Well, interviewers certainly do not appreciate waiting for you either! If there are extenuating circumstances, hopefully not, that leaves some interpretation to this rule. However given no extenuating circumstances, show up at your scheduled time.

Training

I have my degree and lots of related experience. So what is this training requirement thing? Changing careers? Training will definitely be required. Some industries such as Trucking and Airlines will require that you pay for your own depending on your function. Airlines will require many hours and ratings for their new pilots. Flight Attendants and other positions may require some non-paid training. Have you always longed to be on the high road? Maybe a career as a Truck Driver is for you. Be prepared to pay for your training. However, make sure your chosen school will help you get that long awaited job. In addition to researching any required training, do some research on that career? Why, you ask? Before you spend any money on training, check out the library, speak to people in the business, or visit Google or BING to learn about this new career choice. During your research, you might decide this new career choice is not for you. Don't get discouraged. Continue on your search. You might just find the career **you** have longed for.

Travel

Many times one of the decision makers will be in another state or city than you. Therefore, you will be required to travel for an interview. Make sure you understand who will be paying for this and how. Some ads make say mandatory interview to meet CEO in New York, no exceptions, company will not pay for this initial interview. This is even better when the company is in the travel industry. Oh you might ask is that a new way for them to make money – by interviewing lots of out of state candidates.

Travel Requirements

Many sales jobs will state travel required. They may even show a percentage. What would you assume if you saw 70% to 80% travel required? You would probably see yourself building up those frequent flyer miles with many nights away from home. Don't be afraid to ask where. Some employers consider travel as visiting the many customer locations in your local city.

Trenches

Welcome to the war of finding a job. Learn to utilize the military war tactics – you will need them in your job search. They are: don't show your cards, keep a low profile, etc. The reason our Armed Forces build their individualized trenches is first be safe and secondly to have an advantage with the ongoing enemy! You want to secure your safety. You want to secure your added edge by knowing your enemy. The best tactic you may choose to use would be to keep your mouth quiet and don't tell folks your plans. Unfortunately, folks tend to route for the underdog. If being the underdog turns into your giving the perception that you have something in the works that will enhance your life, folks won't consider you the underdog anymore. Folks cannot read your mind. If you go about your everyday business, that's a good thing. If you choose to start bringing in folks that promise not to say anything about your job search, well, you haven't covered your trench very carefully. It's time that you focus on your needs quietly. The folks who stay in their trenches survive! Start planning your job search and then begin implementing your tactics with your end in mind. Remember, safety first! Don't jeopardize your immediate job for the hope of better job tomorrow. You can lead yourself to your next step without jeopardizing anything if you remember to keep within your designated trench!

Trials

Perhaps not with a jury! You will go through many trials with your potential employers, trials within yourself and where you want to be, etc., all parts of life, so do not worry as you go through this phase.

Tribulations

The Dictionary states, -1- "Great affliction, trial, or distress; suffering: "Their tribulation has finally passed. –2- An experience that tests one's endurance, patience, or faith. Ever wonder if we were not given challenges that were set before us, how could we grow and learn and become better? Tribulations are needed to have a full life. If all we had was chocolate and didn't eat any vegetables, well, you get the drift here! We need challenges so we can appreciate all the joy!

Truth

Or consequences? Your resume must reflect the truth. The resume is your marketing tool so you can slant information, avoid information, but never lie.

Tweet

As in that famous cute little yellow bird? Not you? On Twitter you can build and expand your network with many who are considered loose connections. After you get folks following you, Tweet away. Only 140 characters allowed so make your Tweet short and sweet. Getting the word out about whom you are and the areas of expertise you have to offer is a great way to advertise yourself. The good news here is your connections can be as narrow as the executives you'd like to work with or as broad as bloggers in your field or areas of interest. Unlike Facebook or Linked In, Twitter follow or are followed by those they don't interact with in person and may not even know. Job recruiters are browsing on Twitter. Celebrities are on Twitter. Everyone seems to be Tweeting. Everyone is watching so make sure your Tweets build your reputation favorably. In this instant means of communication, if a company has tweeted about a job a minute ago they are most likely stating that the job is available now. So dear job hunters, Tweet away! But be careful what you say – one never knows who may be following you.

$\mathcal{U}$

Underdog

Candidates – no hope? Don't believe that. Now is the time to give you a real pep talk! If you were a Hiring Manager, would you hire you? OF COURSE you would! Now, jot down on a piece of paper all that you bring to the table. What are your specialties? What have you already proven that you do well? What examples can you list regarding your outstanding accomplishments? You might feel as though you fit into the category of, "Underdog", because of your employment status. You are in no way an Underdog; you just don't have a job at this moment in time. You have the power to change your paradigm and become your best promoter, which, of course, is you! One of the biggest lessons learned when feeling as if you are the Underdog, stay away from negative people. It's very contagious to listen to people who share their "chicken little, the sky is falling" mentality. "Yes you can", should become your mantra, just as in the story of the "Little Engine that could"!

Underwear

Many Moms' have asked if you are wearing clean underwear. You need to not only wear clean underwear, but you need to wear clean clothes, clean shoes, and have clean hair. Think about how you want someone to look if you were doing a television interview!

Under Qualified

Or are you really under qualified? Is it because you came across as threatening to the hiring manager? Could this term be used in not hiring you?

V

VC's

Who are they? An illness? How can they help me? Do they have $$$? VC's are Venture Capital Firms. These are the folks who fund new companies. Of course, nothing succeeds like success! Getting involved with VC's and if the idea rockets off to a great start, wow! To begin a new idea with backers putting up the cash and the idea takes off is the ideal position. However, if you have ever visited Las Vegas, every spin doesn't create a win. Winning is much more palatable than losing, as in a sure bet for a VC start up business. However, do we not all agree that sometimes taking a risk might not offer only a winning outcome? Just be cognizant that a start up firm can wind up being a winner or a loser. Keep an open mind regarding the possibility of a winning or losing outcome.

Verbatim

What does this really mean? Some interviews may be conducted in this manner. Don't fall asleep as you find the interviewer reading a script to you. This one could lead to the job of your dreams.

Vibes

What??? You will get these in your first interview encounter – listen to them. Hello! I need you – what are you feeling?

Video Interview

This is a step up from a phone interview and not as personal as an in person interview. Many companies are choosing this option to save time and money. Look at yourself and your surroundings for this video in the mirror. Do you look professional? Do you have a smile on your face? Can you establish what appears to be eye contact? Don't forget to leave a lasting impression. This interview can and will be replayed after it is over.

Voicemail

Rules-learn about the systems before you hit *D. Believe it or not, Voicemail works when used properly! If folks leave a message only stating their name and reach number, that's not the true purpose of having a voice mailbox available. Playing telephone tag is not the best way to utilize this device. BEFORE you leave a voice mail message, write down exactly what you want to say, as succinctly as possible, and then rehearse! When you call whomever, and the line goes into voice mail, you are 100% prepared to leave your message. Of course you would begin by identifying yourself and then you will say the purpose of your call, leaving the recipient of your message want to hear what you have to say. If you are replying to a job ad, state the job ad and how YOU can ease the pain of the person listening to your message. "What's in it for the person listening to your message?" should be the key for your message. Why does the recipient want to call you back? That's how you should plan your voice mail!

Volunteer

As in charity? Where do I begin? How will this help me get a paying job? This is an easy question to answer: NETWORKING! The more people you get to know the better chances you have for locating an open position. In fact, it's even possible to have a new position open for you once your new networking folks find out what you bring to their business.

W

Wages

Wages are not just dollars. Wages combine various and sundry items. When talking about wages, after you are officially offered the position, you must decide on things like, will it cost more money to drive to the new location, will it cost money for parking, are rising gasoline prices leaving you with the feeling that you have another mortgage to pay? At your previous position, or current position, are you receiving more vacation days that what your perspective Employer is offering? Are there personal days offered as well as pay for sick days? All these things will come under the umbrella of, "Wages". After the many screenings of interviews that you have had, and after you have been offered the job, your respective Employer has already invested time and money in finding you for the right person for their job. You are in a great position! It's almost expected that you will not accept the first dollar amount they offer you. If you do accept, you just might give the impression that you were too easy to accept and it will leave a taste of desperation on your part. Should the weekly dollar amount stay the same, without any room for improvement, the other items will certainly be negotiable. Don't sell yourself short! They want you, they have made you an offer, and they would not be willing to have you walk without some sort of negotiation, under the topic of, "Wages".

Wanted

As in the Post Office? You will not feel wanted at all some days as you send off letter after letter. Then one day everyone will call all at once. Hiring Managers will call that you gave up on.

Just remember it is always the darkest before the dawn. Remember, you are in a position where you have a position and you are looking to change your work life to a better work life. First and foremost, do not panic! You could possibly have many feelers out there in the job force and you just never know what is lurking behind the next corner! The economic law of 'supply and demand' is with you! You are currently employed and therefore you are wanted! Hiring Managers always want a challenge and they know you have a job. Having a current position makes you very marketable so your supply chain is not against you! It is now your turn to figure out what YOU want, and not the other way around! When you decide exactly what you want and you figure out all your specifics, for example, job location, salary, job function, and so on, you can then work on finding that spot where your criteria may be met! Have you even given much thought to actually having a job where you would be looking forward to a Monday? This is what your action item is: you are looking for a job you want. You are looking for a job where the powers-that-be want you! Now you can do your research and find the win-win solution to your next job. Yes you can, yes you will, and yes, you can find contentment at your next position!

Watch

Be aware during your interview of clues; be aware of false advertising, etc. Here's where taking on the personae of an ostrich is not in your best interest. The more you 'stop, watch, and listen', the more you will understand your market, what positions are open, what to look for and what are untruths. The first rule of thumb, as you begin using your watchful eye, is don't believe everything you read, especially on job ads! If you choose to only have selected vision, you just might wind up signing up for something that may cost you money. Remember, watch for those enticing ads where if something is too good to be true, then it is too good to be true! As you enter your job search, watch carefully what is not said! If you choose only to watch for the good things, those bad things will be over looked and you will be certainly not a happy camper! If you watch everything you need to watch and see what there is to both see and not see, you will be far ahead of the game!

Websites

Everywhere – how do I start – help! First take a deep, cleansing breath! You will begin your job search by having an open mind and be willing to learn. Here's where becoming humble, and not being arrogant, will help you immensely. By asking questions and listening to the answers would be a great start with your process of utilizing the web. Have you tried using Yahoo! or Google to search for anything? If not, this would be a great time to click on either search engine and look up things that would be of interest to you. Look up Companies that you know. See what their Web Sites are saying. There's information that is merely a click away at your command! Work in incremental steps. Focus on one topic and follow through with just that one topic. Do not allow yourself to be overwhelmed with all the information available to you on the Web. Whatever did we do when the Web was not so attainable? Remember when the libraries were full of folks looking up different subjects and topics? You can perform your own library tasks by learning and using the Web. Ignorance is not bliss! Knowledge is power! You will be able to learn more about almost anything then you ever thought possible! Becoming web friendly will open a new door of adventure and learning to you. One piece of caution: Once you post your information on the web, don't be surprised if Companies scanning these sites will use your information to sell to you something! For example, a Company will contact you after they realize that you are looking for a sales position. This particular Company will try to have you sell their product for a small amount of money, having you do their selling without them paying you a decent wage! Remember, just because someone poses something to you, there are two answers you may give. Those two answers consist of a "yes" or a "no"! You don't have to accept crumbs from others. Stick to your focal point and don't settle for others little crumbs.

What Now?

What resources are there for me? What do they want here? A dynamic personality, willingness to work hand, and a desire to be successful are all prerequisites! What are they really trying to say here? Due to the technical nature of our products and services, multi-level marketing is not available or permitted.

Win-Win

Of course! You will! Just keep the faith!

Why?

In an interview one of the first questions you will always be asked is "So why are you looking? Are you still employed at X Company?" Be positive – Don't say things such as I hate my boss, I hate my job, and I got laid off because they were out to get me. What you never want to do is bad mouth your previous Company and the folks with whom you worked. Whatever negative statement you would make would have your interviewer take the side of their Management. It is the best thing for you to prepare a statement that would address why you are looking for another position. In these times of downsizing, right-sizing, off-shoring, out-sourcing, and budget balancing, most likely you are not the anomaly in the job search market today. Here's where you have the opportunity to say, for example, "My Company offered me a great buy-out package and I now have the opportunity to change fields and be part of another Industry". With your statement, you will give an appropriate answer to the question of, "Why are you looking for another position".

Work Where?

Indiana? India? Virtual Office, no office? Don't be afraid to ask before it is too late. From home jobs, commuting distances versus relocation. Prior to applying for work at home jobs – freeze your bank account! Here's where the old saying of, "If something is too good to be true, then it's too good to be true"! Many work from home jobs offer the best of the best! However, after reading the small print, and after you realize that you must give the ad your charge card number, it is then you realize that this perfect work from home job is a sales ploy to have you purchase something from this ad. Too many times a work from home job is really buying the advertisers' "how to" books and it's really not even a job that is being offered. Purchasing their goods and services is their methodology on how to increase their profits, certainly not your profits. Learn to be a smart consumer. Read everything possible before ever sharing your credit card information. Becoming street savvy is not a bad thing, but by teaching yourself to be questioning of various offers, you can only pat yourself on your back when you pick up a scam or two.

Wreckage?

You've been surplused. Do you feel like wreckage? You respond to a job posting for a regulatory reporting coordinator and have not heard from them. You call them and leave a Voice Mail on their general number. You then send an email to a Manager who works there and ask if there anyone in particular you should call. You then receive a response that your resume had been forwarded internally and should there be any interest they will contact you directly. Of course be aware that we will not be looking to take all of XYZ Company's wreckage and we are primarily looking for those with sales experience. ZZ Communications does thank you for your interest. This is a testimony of the value we bring to the communities we serve in addition to the deployment of new technologies and fair pricing policies. How can you respond? I was pretty sure my expertise was not in your area (sales). I've never been called "wreckage" before, but thanks anyway . . .

X-ray Machines In Buildings

What do I wear on my interview to avoid problems? Nothing? Today's standard of having precautionary measures while entering and exiting a building is more the norm than not. Knowing that you will be going to an unknown building, let's presume that you will be entering a secured building. Now would be a good time to either clear out your pockets and pocket book with things like scissors, or something that could possibly signal a monitoring device. If you can mitigate your nerves as you enter a building by taking away questionable articles, this will save you much angst before you even begin your interview. Pretend that you were going to board an airplane and only bring to your interview things that would be permitted on an airplane. Any thing that you can control, that's what you should do! You certainly don't want to be in a situation where you have to be held up for emptying out the contents of your attaché case, pockets, and/or pocket book.

Yacht Interviews

Wear white-soled shoes and be prepared to get a little sea sick, not from the water but from those who Interview you!

Yellow Pages

How do I use them or can I? Believe it or not, your Yellow Pages can prove to be one of your best friends! How? Quietly, sit in a comfortable chair, in a lighted area, and have the newest version of your Yellow Pages in your geographic area in your hands. As you go through each Industry, not only will the Industries be put in the forefront of your thinking, but also there just might be Industries that you would have never thought about if it weren't for this publication! You will be able to capture what is physically in your living area and you will have their telephone numbers available as well! You can begin your job search with new ideas that you probably would not have thought about at all. You can set up informational interviews. You can get the address and phone number of your local Chamber of Commerce. You will find an infinite number of local businesses that would very well fit into your expertise. "Let your fingers do the walking"!

You

YAHOO! **Y**ou **A**lways **H**ave **O**ther **O**ptions – believe that, because it's true! You do not have to paint yourself in any corner. You have been in difficult situations in your past and some how you found yourself with various ways to make everything work out ok. In the time of job search, remember, it will take one job to fulfill your need. "Gray skies are gonna clear up, put on a happy face"! It's now your turn to help yourself. When folks find out that you have time on your hands, many folks find it very easy to ask you to do personal favors; i.e., go to the grocery store, go to the cleaners, go to the bank, etc. Here's where the word, "No" comes in. You don't have to be rude, but you can say you have a previous appointment. YOU are the previous appointment. Your time should now be spent on you. You're the one searching for a job.

Young

Feel it, be it! Chronological numbers are one thing, but your emotional numbers are what you decide your age should be! You are controlling your food intake, your daily exercise, and your sleep patterns. All these things may help you to feel young. You have kept up with today's happenings. You listen and watch the news, you hear your friend's opinions on various topics, and your state of mind can be dominated with your feeling young and vibrant. Youth and vitality is more then a year of birth. It is a positive state of mind! You have a choice of accepting the youthful persona and as you think it, you will feel it as well as be it!

Z

Zebra

We're all different, even zebras! Did you know that zebras all have different stripes, unique to each one? You are unique! You have different attributes that would bring great things to a new position. Become a zebra, unique and special, and think all good things that you bring and how proud you will feel about seeking out your new position.

Zero

Back to nothing – now what? You are certainly allowed to own your feelings. If you feel that you are truly back to zero, perhaps it's time to revamp your focus. Learning is power! You have experienced many new scenarios within your job search. Should you feel that you are back to zero, well, that's just not the case at all! Give yourself a pat on your back for all you have learned. Think about all the folks you have met through your job search. Would you really consider yourself back to "zero"?

Zipper

Prior to arriving at an interview make sure it is closed if you have one! Prior to your interview, take a few moments to stop and do a quick check on your physical togetherness. Whether it be checking a zipper to ensure it's closure, or checking your teeth from left over spinach, it's a good idea to be prepared and make sure your physical appearance will not leave you embarrassed in regard to how you look!

Zoo

What a ----------!! Can you remember when you first visited a zoo? Do you remember all the different animals that were there? Can you recall the different personalities of each species that you encountered? Now, try to pretend that in your visit to an office where you have never been before as you meet with a Hiring Manager for a perspective new job. Can you pretend you are back at the zoo? You are now in a new situation with new species for you to meet and win over! How different is this than your visit to a zoo? Keep that thought to yourself and you will keep your humor and much needed sanity.

The Alphabetized Job Search

Index

A   3

Activity   3
Ads   3
Age   4
Agenda   5
Agreeable   5
Allergies   5
Analyze   6
Anger   6
Animals   7
Applications   7
Apple   8
Applying   8
Are   9
Art   10
Assess   10
Attitude   11

B   13

Baggage   13
Begging   13
Beginning   13
Behavioral Questions   14
Believe   15
Be Prepared   15
BIAS   15
Bizarre   16
Blitz   16
BLOGS   17
Boring   17
Breathe   17
Breathing   18

Bullet Points   18
Business Plan   19
Busy   19

C   20

Calendar   20
Call Center Jobs   20
Callbacks   21
Calling   21
Calm   22
Cars   22
Cattle Calls   23
Clarification   23
Clothes   23
Compensation   24
Complacent   24
Computer   25
Confirmations   25
Connections   25
Continue   26
Control   26
Cookies   27
Cover Letters, E-Mails   27
Credit Checks   28

D   29

Dates   29
Dealing With All This Stuff   29
Degree   30
Direct Mail   30
Directions   31
Discrimination   31
Distance   32
DNA   32
Do's & Don'ts   33
Dressing For Interviews   33
Duck   34
Duct Tape   34

Dueling For Jobs	34
E	36
Easy	36
Ego	36
E-Mail Interviews	36
Emotions	37
English	37
Enthusiasm	38
Entry-Level Jobs	38
Expectations	39
Extra, Extra, Read All About It!	39
F	40
Failure	40
Faxing	40
Feelings	40
Film	40
Finding	41
Flexible Hours	41
Flirting	41
Fluent	41
Flying	42
Focus	42
Freedom	42
Friday	43
Friends	43
Frog	44
Fun	44
Funny Names	45
G	46
Ganging Up	46
Games Played	47
Gap	47
Glass Doors	48
Goals	48
GOD	49

Government Jobs 49
GPA 49
Great Feeling 49
Grey Hair 50
GUT 50

H 51

Hair 51
Hand Shake 51
Hanging 51
Headhunters 52
Help 52
Hiding Info 52
Hidden Agenda 53
Hiring Manager 53
Homework 53
Hotel interviews 54
How 54
HR 54

I 55

Identity Theft 55
In Demand 55
Informational Meetings 55
Inside Sales 56
Interview 56
Interviewing 57
Inventions 57

J 58

Jerks 58
Job Ads 58
Job Applications 60
Job Boards 60
Joking While Looking 61
Joining Professional Chat Groups 61
Joy 61
Judging & Judges 62

	Jungle	62
	Justify	62
K		63
	Kindness	63
	Know-It-All	63
	Knowledge	63
	Know Thy Self	63
L		65
	Landing On Your Feet	65
	Language	65
	Late Hours	65
	Legalities	65
	Lessons Learned	65
	Likeability Factor	65
	Listen	66
	Listings	66
	Looks	66
	Love It Or Leave It	67
	Low-Level Job Surprises In Your Interview	67
	Luck In An Interview, On The Job Boards	67
M		68
	Magic	68
	Manage	68
	Many	68
	Marketing	68
	Math Tests	69
	Microwave Minutes	69
	Mirroring For A Job	69
	Miserable	69
	Missing Info	70
	Mistakes	70
	Money	71
	Morphing	71
	Motivation	72
	Murphy's Law	73

N   74

     Name   74
     Needs   74
     Negotiate   74
     Networking   75
     Nonsense Job Ads   76
     Notice   76

O   77

     Offer   77
     Old   77
     Overqualified   78
     Overtime   78
     Overwhelmed   79
     Oxymoron   79

P   80

     Paper   80
     Passion   80
     People   80
     Personalities   81
     Phone Interviews   81
     Phone Numbers   82
     Phony   82
     Plan B   82
     Politics   83
     Pool   83
     Predicting   83
     Presentations   84
     Prey   84
     Professionalism   84

Q   86

     Qualifications   86
     Qualities   86
     Queries   87
     Quickly   87

R   88

    Rambling   88
    Reality   88
    Reading   89
    Red Flags   89
    Referrals   90
    References   90
    Regret Letters   90
    Rehearsing   91
    Reinvent Yourself   91
    Rejection   92
    Requirements   92
    Relocation   93
    Restaurant Interviews   93
    Resumes   94
    Ringer   95
    Rip Off's   95
    Risks   95
    Rolodex   95
    Rules   96

S   97

    School Of Hard Knocks   97
    Screen   97
    Search Engines   97
    Seasoned   98
    Secretaries   98
    Selling Short   99
    Serendipity   100
    Settling   100
    Side Jobs   100
    Signs   101
    Silence   101
    Skills   101
    Small World   101
    SOAR   102
    Sorting   102

Speaking   103
Spell Check   103
Spirit   104
Stick To Your Knitting   104
Stimulus   105
Stood Up   105
Study   105
Squares   105
Successes   106
Sucks   106
Surprises   107

T   108

Telecommuting   108
Telephone Tag   108
Tenacious   109
Terms & Conditions   109
Tests   109
Thank You   110
Thank You Notes   111
Time   111
Training   111
Travel   112
Travel Requirements   112
Trenches   113
Trials   113
Tribulations   114
Truth   114
Tweet   114

U   116

Underdog   116
Underwear   116
Under Qualified   117

V   118

VC's   118
Verbatim   118

Vibes	118
Video Interview	119
Voicemail	119
Volunteer	119
W	**121**
Wages	121
Wanted	122
Watch	122
Websites	123
What Now?	124
Win-Win	124
Why?	124
Work Where?	125
Wreckage?	125
X	**127**
X-ray Machines In Buildings	127
Y	**128**
Yacht Interviews	128
Yellow Pages	128
You	128
Young	129
Z	**130**
Zebra	130
Zero	130
Zipper	130
Zoo	131

www.ingramcontent.com/pod-product-compliance
Lightning Source LLC
Chambersburg PA
CBHW081128170526
45165CB00008B/2596